SpringerBriefs in Computer Science

Series editors

Stan Zdonik
Peng Ning
Shashi Shekhar
Jonathan Katz
Xindong Wu
Lakhmi C. Jain
David Padua
Xuemin Shen
Borko Furht
V. S. Subrahmanian
Martial Hebert
Katsushi Ikeuchi
Bruno Siciliano

For further volumes:
http://www.springer.com/series/10028

Harry Strange · Reyer Zwiggelaar

Open Problems in Spectral Dimensionality Reduction

 Springer

Harry Strange
Department of Computer Science
Aberystwyth University
Aberystwyth
UK

Reyer Zwiggelaar
Department of Computer Science
Aberystwyth University
Aberystwyth
UK

ISSN 2191-5768   ISSN 2191-5776 (electronic)
ISBN 978-3-319-03942-8   ISBN 978-3-319-03943-5 (eBook)
DOI 10.1007/978-3-319-03943-5
Springer Cham Heidelberg New York Dordrecht London

Library of Congress Control Number: 2013956626

Printed on acid-free paper

Springer is part of Springer Science+Business Media (www.springer.com)

Preface

> The ability to simplify means to eliminate the unnecessary
> so that the necessary may speak.
>
> —Hans Hofmann, 1880–1966

The last few years have seen a great increase in the amount of data available to scientists, engineers, and researchers from many disciplines. Datasets with millions of objects and hundreds, if not thousands, of measurements are now commonplace in areas such as image analysis, computational finance, bio-informatics, and astrophysics. This large volume of data does, however, come at a price, more often than not many computational techniques used to analyze these datasets cannot cope with such large data. Therefore, strategies need to be employed as a pre-processing step to reduce the number of objects, or measurements, whilst retaining important information inherent to the data. One of the key problems with such datasets is how to reduce the number of measurements, often referred to as dimensions, in such a way that the reduced set of measurements captures the main properties of the original data. Spectral dimensionality reduction is one such family of methods that has proven to be an indispensable tool in the data processing pipeline. In recent years, the area has gained much attention; thanks to the development of nonlinear spectral dimensionality reduction methods, often referred to as manifold learning algorithms.

Spectral dimensionality reduction methods can be broadly split into two categories; those that seek to maintain linear properties in the data, and those that seek to maintain nonlinear, manifold, properties. Both linear and nonlinear methods achieve the reduction in dimensionality through the careful construction of a feature matrix, the spectral decomposition of which gives rise to the reduced dimensionality dataset. Ever since the first nonlinear spectral dimensionality reduction methods were proposed over a decade ago, numerous algorithms and improvements have been proposed for the purpose of performing spectral dimensionality reduction. Although these algorithms may improve and extend existing techniques, there is still no gold standard technique. The reasons for this are many; however, one of the core problems with the area is that there are still many obstacles that need to be overcome before spectral dimensionality reduction that can be applied to a specific problem area. These obstacles, referred to herein

v

as *open problems*, have implications for those without a background in the area who wish to employ spectral dimensionality reduction to their problem domain.

Those wish to use spectral dimensionality reduction without prior knowledge of the field will immediately be confronted with questions that need answering; what parameter values to use? how many dimensions should the data be embedded into? how are new data points incorporated? what about large-scale data? For many, a search of the literature to find answers to these questions is impractical, as such, there is a need for a concise discussion into the problems themselves, how they affect spectral dimensionality reduction and how these problems can be overcome.

This book provides a survey and reference aimed at advanced undergraduate and postgraduate students as well as researchers, scientists, and engineers in a wide range of disciplines. Dimensionality reduction has proven useful in a wide range of problem domains, and so this book will be applicable to anyone with a solid grounding in statistics and computer science seeking to apply spectral dimensionality to their work.

Acknowledgments

We both would like to thank the love and support of Jo, Diana, and our families. As well as to this, we would like to acknowledge both NISCHR and the Aberystwyth APRS funding schemes for partially supporting this work.

Aberystwyth, October 2013   Harry Strange
                                                               Reyer Zwiggelaar

Contents

Chapter 1
Introduction

Abstract A brief introduction to dimensionality reduction and manifold learning is provided and supported by a visual example. The goals of the book and its place in the literature is given, while the chapter is concluded by an outline of the remainder of the book.

Keywords Manifold learning · Spectral dimensionality reduction · Medical image analysis

Many problems in the machine learning, computer vision, and pattern recognition domains are inherently high-dimensional, that is, the number of measurements taken per observation is considered 'high'. There are both practical and theoretical reasons for wanting to reduce the number of measurements to a more manageable amount. One such motivating factor is that visualising information that contains more than three dimensions is a near impossible task. Although methods have been presented to aid in multi-variate visualisation, humans are still limited to visualising data in three dimensions or less. As such, reducing the number of measurements, or dimensionality, of a dataset is an important process when seeking to visually analyse and understand the data. From a theoretical perspective, high-dimensional spaces have a number of properties that can pose real difficulties. The well known "curse of dimensionality" [1] and "empty space problem" [2] are two examples of such difficulties; as the number of dimensions increases, the properties often associated with 2 or 3-dimensional Euclidean spaces disintegrate and are replaced by strange and complex phenomena [3].

Such practical and theoretical motivations drive the need for automatic methods that can reduce the dimensionality of a dataset in an intelligent way. Spectral dimensionality reduction is one such family of methods. Spectral dimensionality reduction seeks to transform the high-dimensional data into a lower dimensional space that retains certain properties of the subspace or sub manifold upon which the data lies. This transformation is achieved via the spectral decomposition of a square symmetric feature matrix. This spectral decomposition step is what separates such methods from other manifold learning approaches such as Autoencoders [4], Manifold Sculpting [5], Stochastic Neighbor Embedding [6], and Curvilinear Components Analysis [7]. Spectral dimensionality reduction methods have proved useful in numerous application areas including speech analysis [8], digital histology [9], analysis of microarray data [10], and face recognition [11]. However, in such applications, there are many considerations that need to be taken into account prior to using spectral dimensionality reduction.

Consider as an example a set of MRI and Ultrasound prostate images taken from a selection of different patients. For each image a binary segmentation that corresponds to the boundary of the prostate region is taken (Fig. 1.1c). A set of 252 features are then extracted from each segmentation image using a multi resolution hierarchical feature extraction approach [12]. Each image can therefore be represented as a vector in 252-dimensional space. The variation between each image is much smaller than the number of features; so although the number of features per image is high, there is a large amount of redundancy. In fact, the images are expected to lie on or near a low-dimensional manifold parameterised by the shape of the prostate. Therefore, performing spectral dimensionality reduction on this set of points in 252-dimensional feature space will return a more compact low-dimensional representation of the data which maintains the shape variation between the images. Figure 1.1a shows the result of performing spectral dimensionality reduction, in this case Locality Preserving Projections (LPP) [13], on this set of data. As can be seen, the 3-dimensional representation of the data reveals the changes in shape of the prostate with each axis of the low-dimensional space corresponding to a different 'shape change'.

To obtain the low-dimensional embedding shown in Fig. 1.1 many decisions had to be made along the way. First and foremost, which dimensionality reduction algorithm to use had to be decided upon. Then, since a graph based method was chosen, a neighbourhood size value had to be selected alongside a target dimensionality. Although not mentioned above, further problems could present themselves if new images were to be added to the previously learnt embedding, or the total number of images grew to a large amount. Each of these decisions and problems can be related back to the assumptions that are made both by the user, and by the spectral dimensionality reduction algorithm, about the problem domain. It is these problems and assumptions that often prevent spectral dimensionality reduction to be effectively used. Since there are no standard solutions to many of these problems they remain 'open problems', and it is on these problems that this book is focused.

1.1 Goals of the Book

The purpose of this book is to organise and directly address some of the key problems that are associated with spectral dimensionality reduction. As already mentioned, all of these problems arise from certain assumptions made either by spectral dimensionality reduction algorithms, or users of these algorithms, about the problem domain.

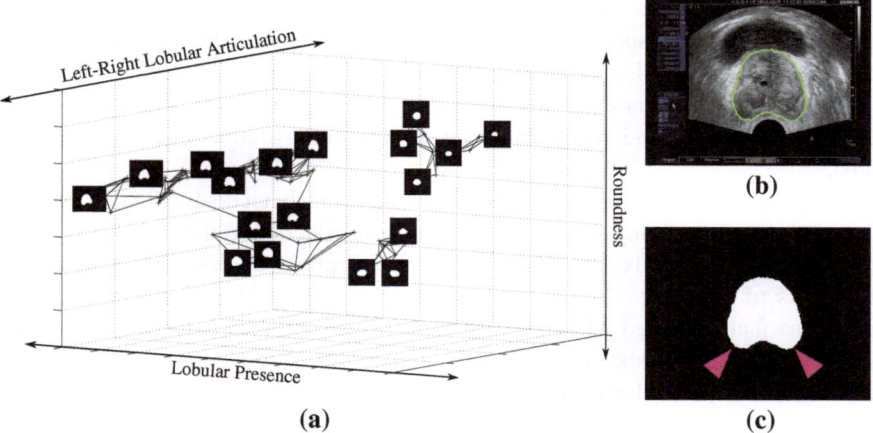

Fig. 1.1 Example embedding of a shape manifold of multiple MRI and ultrasound prostate images (**a**). The prostate boundary is segmented from the images, in this case an Ultrasound image (**b**), and features such as the presence and articulation of lobes, as shown by the *arrows* in (**c**), vary along each of the dimensions of the low-dimensional embedding

As such, there is a lively interplay between the algorithms themselves, the general setting within which they are framed, the assumptions that specific algorithms make, and the problems that arise from such assumptions. This book can therefore be used as a reference for those seeking to quickly understand spectral dimensionality reduction and the potential solutions to various problems. It can also serve as an introduction to the field for those new to spectral dimensionality reduction.

1.2 Relation to Existing Work

Over the last few years, spectral dimensionality reduction has gained much attention with many excellent reviews of the leading algorithms being presented. The seminal work in this field is 'Nonlinear Dimensionality Reduction' by Lee and Verleysen [3]. Their book provides a detailed presentation and discussion of many of the leading approaches to nonlinear dimensionality reduction. Although thorough, Lee and Verleysen's book is not suitable for those without a solid background within the field. As a reference, it is only useful to those with a solid grounding in linear algebra, machine learning, and topology. As well as this, the problems associated with applying such algorithms are not dealt with in any real detail.

Another important review is that of van der Maaten et al. [14] who provide a concise, yet detailed description of leading techniques for dimensionality reduction. Their chapter is far more condensed than that of Lee and Verleysen and so serves as a good guide and reference to dimensionality reduction techniques. The focus of the chapter is very much on the algorithms themselves rather than issues related to employing them. As such, open problems are rarely discussed with the exception being the out-of-sample extension.

Other review papers exist [15–20] but none of these papers are aimed at non-experts who wish to understand and apply dimensionality reduction to their problem area.

This book differs from the aforementioned books in that it deals with the problems associated with applying spectral dimensionality reduction, rather than focusing on the algorithms themselves. Although leading algorithms are described, they are not the focus of the book. Rather, the focus is on how to address and overcome the problems that are faced when using spectral dimensionality reduction. This focus seeks to make this book useful for a wide audience of researchers, scientists, and engineers who do not have a background in the area.

1.3 Outline

The remainder of this book is structured as follows. In Chap. 2, a mathematical setting for spectral dimensionality reduction is presented along with some of the leading linear and nonlinear algorithms. Chapter 3 is the first of the four open problems chapters and introduces the problems associated with modelling the underlying manifold upon which the data is assumed to lie. Chapter 4 deals with problems associated with intrinsic dimensionality such as estimation of intrinsic dimensionality and embeddings into spaces with 'high' dimensionality. Chapter 5 deals with the problem of incorporating new points into previously learnt embeddings which is an important problem to solve if using spectral dimensionality reduction for classification problems. Chapter 6 presents problems and potential solutions associated with using spectral dimensionality reduction on large scale data. Finally, Chap. 7 provides a brief discussion of the wider setting of spectral dimensionality reduction along with some conclusions.

References

1. Bellman, R.: Adaptive Control Processes: A Guided Tour. Princeton University Press (1961)
2. Scott, D.W., Thompson, J.R.: Probablitiy density estimation in higher dimensions. In: J.R. Gentle (ed.) Proceedings of the Fifteenth Symposium on the Interface, pp. 173–179 (1983)
3. Lee, J.A., Verleysen, M.: Nonlinear Dimensionality Reduction. Springer (2007)
4. Hinton, G.E., Salakhutdinov, R.R.: Reducing the dimensionality of data with neural networks. Science **313**, 504–507 (2006)
5. Gashler, M., Ventura, D., Martinez, T.: Iterative non-linear dimensionality reduction by manifold sculpting. In: Advances in Neural Information Processing Systems 20: Proceedings of the 2008 Conference (NIPS) (2008)

6. Hinton, G., Roweis, S.: Stochastic Neighbor Embedding. In: Advances in Neural Information Processing Systems 15: Proceedings of the 2003 Conference (NIPS), pp. 833–840. MIT Press (2000)
7. Demartines, P., Herault, J.: Curvilinear component analysis: A self-organizing neural network for nonlinear mapping of data sets. IEEE Transactions on Neural Networks **8**(1), 148–154 (1997)
8. Jansen, A., Niyogi, P.: Intrinsic spectral analysis. IEEE Transactions on Signal Processing (to appear) **61**(1), 1698–1710 (2013)
9. Arif, M., Rajpoot, N.: Classification of potential nuclei in prostate histology images using shape manifold learning. In: Proceedings of the 2007 International Conference on Machine Vision, pp. 113–118 (2007)
10. Teng, L., Li, H., Fu, X., Chen, W., Shen, I.F.: Dimension reduction of microarray data based on local tangent space alignment. In: Proceedings of the 4th IEEE International Conference on Cognitive Informatics, pp. 154–159 (2005)
11. He, X., Yan, S., Hu, Y., P.Niyogi, Zhang, H.J.: Face recognition using laplacianfaces. IEEE Transactions on Pattern Analysis and Machine Intelligence **27**(3), 328–340 (2005)
12. Park, J., Govindaraju, V., Srihari, S.N.: OCR in a hierarchical feature space. IEEE Transactions on Pattern Analysis and Machine Intelligence **22**(4), 400–407 (2000)
13. He, X., Niyogi, P.: Locality Preserving Projections. In: Advances in Neural Information Processing Systems 16: Proceedings of the 2003 Conference (NIPS), pp. 153–160. MIT Press (2003)
14. van der Maaten, L., Postma, E., van den Herik, J.: Dimensionality reduction: A comparitive review. Tech. Rep. TiCC-TR 2009–005, Tilburg University (2009). Unpublished
15. Fodor, I.K.: A survery of dimension reduction techniques. Tech. Rep. UCRL-ID-148, US Department of, Energy (2002)
16. Ma, Y., Fu, Y.: Manifold Learning Theory and Applications. CRC Press (2012)
17. Mysling, P., Hauberg, S., Pedersen, K.S.: An empirical study on the performance of spectral manifold learning techniques. In: Proceedings of the 21th international conference on Artificial neural networks - Volume Part I, ICANN'11, pp. 347–354 (2011)
18. Saul, L.K., Weinberger, K.Q., Ham, J.H., Sha, F., Lee, D.D.: Semisupervised Learning, chap. Spectral Methods for Dimensionality Reduction, pp. 293–308. MIT Press, Cambridge, MA (2006)
19. Pless, R., Souvenir, R.: A survey of manifold learning for images. IPSJ Transactions on Computer Vision and Applications **1**, 83–94 (2009)
20. Vlachos, M., Domeniconi, C., Gunopulos, D., Kollios, G., Koudas, N.: Non-linear dimensionality reduction techniques for classification and visualization. In: Proceedings of the eigth ACM SIGKDD Interenational Conference on Knowledge Discovery and Data Mining, pp. 645–651 (2002)

Chapter 2
Spectral Dimensionality Reduction

Abstract In this chapter a common mathematical framework is provided which forms the basis for subsequent chapters. Generic aspects are covered, after which specific dimensionality reduction approaches are briefly described.

Keywords Spectral dimensionality reduction algorithms · Kernel methods · Spectral graph theory.

Before addressing the open problems it is important to have an understanding of the problem domain itself along with the techniques that have been proposed to perform spectral dimensionality reduction. To fully understand and appreciate the open problems they need to be described in terms of a common mathematical framework. By doing so the problems described in the latter sections can be coherently addressed in relation to a common frame of reference.

This section begins by providing a general mathematical setting within which both spectral dimensionality reduction, and the associated open problems, can be described. Then key algorithms, both linear and nonlinear, are briefly described so as to provide an important point of reference and discussion for the later discussion of open problems.

2.1 A General Setting for Spectral Dimensionality Reduction

To effectively analyse spectral dimensionality reduction and the associated problems it is useful to frame the methodology within a general setting. As the name suggests, at the heart of spectral dimensionality reduction is the spectral decomposition of a square symmetric feature matrix. Different techniques can be distinguished based on the construction of this feature matrix and the eigenvectors that are subsequently used (i.e. smallest or largest). This feature matrix aims to capture certain properties of the

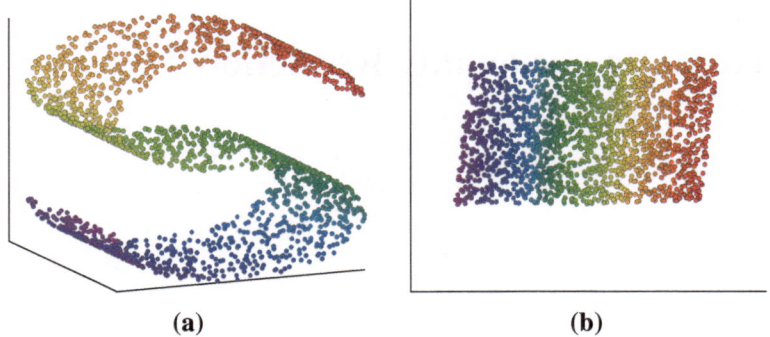

Fig. 2.1 The S-Curve dataset (**a**) along with its low-dimensional embedding (**b**)

subspace or submanifold upon which the data lies, the spectral decomposition of this matrix then gives rise to the low-dimensional embedding (Fig. 2.1). With this in mind the general setting of spectral dimensionality reduction can be defined as follows:

Definition 1 *Given a set of D-dimensional data* $\mathbf{X} = \{\mathbf{x}_i\}_{i=1}^n \in \mathbb{R}^D$ *that is sampled from a d-dimensional manifold* $\mathscr{M}$ *such that* $\mathbf{X} \subset \mathscr{M}$, *the goal of dimensionality reduction is to recover a set of d-dimensional data* $\mathbf{Y} = \{\mathbf{y}_i\}_{i=1}^n \in \mathbb{R}^d$ *(d $\ll$ D) such that* $\mathbf{Y}$ *is a faithful representation of* $\mathbf{X}$ *and preserves certain properties of* $\mathscr{M}$.

Due to the vagueness of this definition, many questions naturally present themselves. For example, what constitutes a faithful representation of the original data? Is the high-dimensional data expected to lie on or near a low-dimensional subspace or a low-dimensional submanifold? How is the data sampled from this subspace or submanifold? These types of questions underlie the general assumptions that different approaches make about the setting within which dimensionality reduction takes place and will be returned to in due course.

A more formal definition of spectral dimensionality reduction can be obtained by "filling in" some of the gaps found in Definition 1. As previously mentioned, a feature matrix is built from $\mathbf{X}$ that aims to capture certain properties of the data and will often represent subspace or submanifold properties. Given the original data $\mathbf{X}$, the feature matrix $\mathbf{F}$ is built such that

(i) $\mathbf{F}$ is a square $n \times n$ matrix. Here n could refer to the number of objects in the dataset or the ambient dimensionality of the data
(ii) $\mathbf{F}$ is symmetric, i.e. $\mathbf{F}_{ij} \equiv \mathbf{F}_{ji}$ $\forall$ $i, j \in [1, \ldots n]$
(iii) $\mathbf{F}$ is positive semi-definite, that is, $\mathbf{u}^T \mathbf{F} \mathbf{u} \geq 0$ for every $\mathbf{u} \in \mathbb{R}^D$

It is this similarity matrix that distinguishes various spectral dimensionality reduction techniques. For example, $\mathbf{F}$ could measure the covariance of $\mathbf{X}$ as in Principal Components Analysis [1], or the geodesic interpoint distances as in Isomap [2].

Once $\mathbf{F}$ has been built, it is recast in terms of its eigenvectors and eigenvalues using eigendecomposition. By decomposing $\mathbf{F}$ in such a manner the low-dimensional representation can be found. Given that $\mathbf{F}$ is a square symmetric matrix, it can be recast as

$$\mathbf{F} = \mathbf{Q}\Lambda\mathbf{Q}^T \tag{2.1}$$

where $\mathbf{Q}$ is a $D \times n$ matrix containing the eigenvectors as columns and Λ is a $n \times n$ matrix with the eigenvalues on the diagonal, assuming that $\mathbf{F}$ is of size $n \times n$. Each eigenvector $\mathbf{u}_i \in \mathbf{Q}$ has a corresponding eigenvalue $\lambda_i \in \Lambda$ for which $\mathbf{F}\mathbf{u}_i = \lambda_i\mathbf{u}_i$. The low-dimensional representation $\mathbf{Y}$ is then found by utilising either the top or bottom eigenvectors of the decomposition of $\mathbf{X}$ found using Eq. (2.1).

2.2 Linear Spectral Dimensionality Reduction

Linear approaches to spectral dimensionality reduction make the assumption that the data lies on or near a low-dimensional subspace. In such cases, linear spectral dimensionality reduction methods seek to 'learn' the basis vectors of this low-dimensional subspace so that the input data can be projected onto the linear subspace. The two main methods for linear spectral dimensionality reduction, Principal Components Analysis and Multidimensional Scaling, are both described in this section. Although more powerful nonlinear approaches have been presented in recent years, these linear techniques are still widely used and are worthy of attention since they provide the basis for some of the subsequent nonlinear spectral dimensionality reduction algorithms.

2.2.1 Principal Components Analysis (PCA)

PCA [1, 3] seeks to find the low-dimensional subspace within the data that maximally preserves the covariance up to rotation. This maximum covariance subspace encapsulates the directions along which the data varies the most. Therefore, projecting the data onto this subspace can be thought of as projecting the data onto the subspace that retains the most information. An example embedding found using PCA is shown in Fig. 2.2a.

The first step of PCA is to calculate the $D \times D$ covariance matrix of $\mathbf{X}$,

$$\mathbf{F} = \frac{1}{n} \sum_{i=1}^{n} \mathbf{x}_i \mathbf{x}_i^T \tag{2.2}$$

with the assumption that $\mathbf{X}$ is centred at the origin (i.e. zero mean). PCA is the only spectral dimensionality reduction technique where the feature matrix $\mathbf{F}$ is not in terms of the number of data points n, but rather the original dimensionality D. The eigendecomposition of $\mathbf{F}$, found according to Eq. (2.1), gives rise to the basis vectors

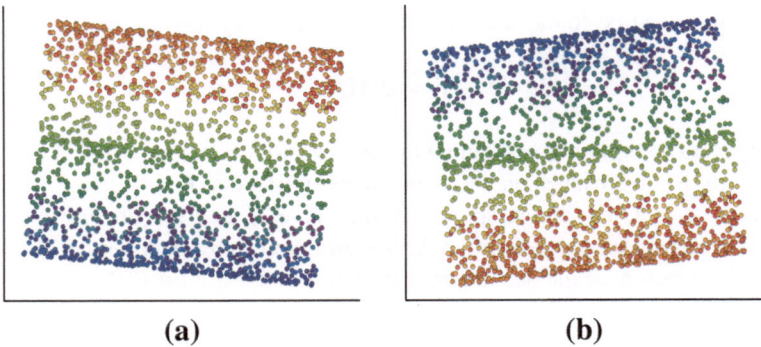

Fig. 2.2 Example 2-dimensional embeddings of the S-Curve dataset found by **a** Principal Components Analysis, and **b** Multidimensional Scaling

of the subspace upon which the data lies on or near. Therefore, the low-dimensional embedding found according to PCA is given by the projection $\mathbf{Y} = \mathbf{XQ}_{1...d}$, where $\mathbf{Q}_{1...d}$ is the matrix of d eigenvectors ordered in descending order of their associated eigenvalues.

The intuition behind PCA is that the largest eigenvector of the matrix $\mathbf{F}$ corresponds to the dimension in the high-dimensional space along which $\mathbf{X}$ varies the most. Similarly, the second largest eigenvector corresponds to the dimension with the second most variation, and so on. So the top d-eigenvectors describe the d-dimensional subspace which contains the most variance.

2.2.2 Classical Multidimensional Scaling (MDS)

Classical MDS [4], sometimes referred to as metric MDS, shares many similar properties to PCA, as shown by the example low-dimensional embedding in Fig. 2.2b. Whereas PCA seeks to find the subspace that maximally preserves variance, MDS seeks to preserve pairwise distances in the low-dimensional space. As such, MDS takes as input a matrix, $\mathbf{S}$, of squared pairwise distances:

$$\mathbf{S}_{ij} = ||\mathbf{x}_i - \mathbf{x}_j||^2 \tag{2.3}$$

The squared distance matrix in its raw form is not positive semi-definite, so cannot be used as the feature matrix for spectral dimensionality reduction. Therefore, it needs to be converted to a Gram, or inner-product, matrix through the following transformation:

$$\mathbf{F} = -\frac{1}{2}\mathbf{HSH} \tag{2.4}$$

where $\mathbf{H}$ is a centring matrix such that $\mathbf{H} = \mathbf{I} - \frac{1}{n}\mathbf{e}\mathbf{e}^T$ where $\mathbf{I}$ is the $n \times n$ identity matrix, and $\mathbf{e}$ is an n vector of all ones. The spectral decomposition of $\mathbf{F}$ gives rise to the top d eigenvalues $\{\lambda_j\}_{j=1}^d$ and eigenvectors $\{\mathbf{q}_j\}_{j=1}^d$. The low-dimensional embedding found according to MDS is then

$$\mathbf{Y} = \left\{\sqrt{\lambda_j}\mathbf{q}_{ji}\right\}_{i=1}^n \tag{2.5}$$

Both PCA and Classical MDS give rise to the same low-dimensional embedding and the Gram matrix (Eq. 2.4) has the same rank and eigenvalues up to a constant factor as the feature (covariance) matrix of PCA [5].

2.3 Nonlinear Spectral Dimensionality Reduction

The central limitation of linear approaches to dimensionality reduction is that they assume the data lies on or near a linear subspace. In practice this may not always be the case; spaces may be locally linear, but unlike the assumption made by linear techniques, globally they may be highly nonlinear. As such, using linear techniques in such circumstances could lead to distorted results with curved areas of the data being projected on top of each other.

Nonlinear spectral dimensionality reduction techniques seek to alleviate this problem by modelling the data not using a subspace, but a submanifold. The data is assumed to be sampled from a low-dimensional manifold embedded within a high-dimensional space. This manifold could be highly nonlinear and convoluted, yet nonlinear methods seek to maintain this manifold structure in the low-dimensional space such that points that are close on the manifold are close in the low-dimensional space, and conversely, points that are far away on the manifold are mapped as far away in the low-dimensional space. An example of this is shown in Fig. 2.3.

In all cases, the feature matrix is built from a graph whose vertices correspond to the input data, and whose edge set corresponds to neighbourhood relations. Therefore, nonlinear spectral dimensionality reduction methods build on the principles laid out in linear algebra and graph theory whereby a graph is reconstructible from its spectrum and the eigenvectors of the graph's adjacency matrix [6].

This section reviews some of the most popular methods for nonlinear spectral dimensionality reduction. This list of methods is by no means exhaustive, rather, the methods included in this section are chosen for their didactic value and also their popularity. Each method corresponds to an important and different paradigm to spectral dimensionality reduction; as such, they are each landmarks within the landscape of spectral dimensionality reduction and provide a brief but sufficient survey of the main trends within this area.

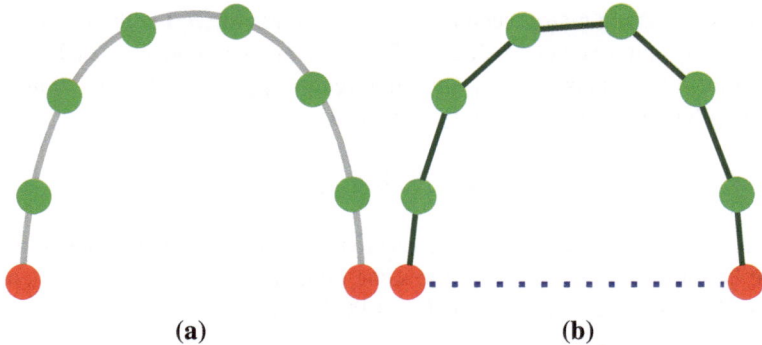

(a)   (b)

Fig. 2.3 Points sampled from a simple horseshoe shaped manifold (**a**). The two distances in (**b**) show the difference between distances as measured across the manifold and the Euclidean distance. The two end points are connected by the *dotted line* according to the Euclidean distance. However, their manifold distance would be the sum of inter-point distances on the path between the two points. For nonlinear spectral dimensionality reduction techniques, the manifold distances should be used so that the two end points are mapped as far away in the low-dimensional space

Fig. 2.4 Example 2-dimensional embeddings of the S-Curve dataset found by Isomap with $k = 12$

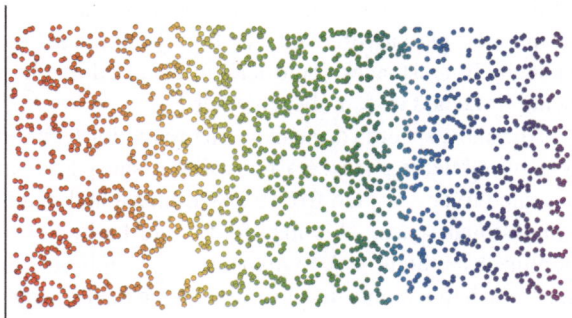

2.3.1 Isomap

Isomap [2], one of the first true nonlinear spectral dimensionality reduction methods, extends metric MDS to handle nonlinear manifolds. Whereas metric MDS measures inter-point Euclidean distances to obtain a feature matrix, Isomap measures the inter-point *manifold* distances by approximating geodesics. The use of manifold distances can often lead to a more accurate and robust measure of distances between points so that points that are far away according to manifold distances, as measured in the high-dimensional space, are mapped as far away in the low-dimensional space (Fig. 2.3). An example low-dimensional embedding of the S-Curve dataset (Fig. 2.1) found using Isomap is given in Fig. 2.4.

At the heart of Isomap is the computation of the manifold inter-point distances which is achieved by estimating the geodesic distances across a neighbourhood graph. The geodesic distance between two points is represented as $\mathbf{S}_{ij} = \phi(\mathbf{x}_i, \mathbf{x}_j)$, where

$\phi(\cdot)$ is the distance between $\mathbf{x}_i$ and $\mathbf{x}_j$ as measured using geodesics. The key insight of Isomap is that the geodesic distance function corresponds to the summation of the distances of 'short-hops' along a neighbourhood graph. Given a graph $G = \langle V, E \rangle$ such that V is the vertex set equal to $\mathbf{X}$, and the edge set E contains the local connectivity of the vertices (calculated by the k-nearest neighbour rule or the ε-neighbourhood rule) the distance $\phi(\mathbf{x}_i, \mathbf{x}_j)$ corresponds to the shortest path in G between vertices $\mathbf{x}_i$ and $\mathbf{x}_j$ as calculated by an algorithm such as Dijkstra's method [7].

As with MDS, the matrix $\mathbf{S}$ is not positive semi-definite, so a Gram matrix is derived according to Eq. (2.4). Once the geodesic distances have been computed, Isomap follows the same algorithm as MDS. The Gram matrix is decomposed into eigenvalues and eigenvectors and the low-dimensional embedding is given by Eq. (2.5). However, unlike MDS, the feature matrix captures manifold distances as opposed to squared Euclidean distances. Therefore, the low-dimensional embedding will maintain manifold properties rather than linear subspace properties.

2.3.2 Maximum Variance Unfolding (MVU)

Sometimes referred to as semidefinite embedding, MVU [8] seeks to find the low-dimensional representation by 'unrolling' the high-dimensional data. As with Isomap, MVU constructs a k-nearest neighbourhood graph to represent the connectivity of the manifold as sampled by the data in $\mathbf{X}$. However, unlike Isomap, spectral decomposition is not performed on this connectivity matrix, rather, the datapoints are unfolded, throughout the formulation of an optimisation problem, by separating the data as much as possible subject to specific constraints. At its core, MVU seeks to maximise the Euclidean distances between the datapoints whilst leaving the distances at a local scale unchanged. This is done by formulating the central optimisation problem as that of a semidefinite program [9].

The solution to the maximum variance unfolding problem is found by constructing a Gram matrix, $\mathbf{F}$, whose top eigenvectors give rise to the low-dimensional representation of the data. MVU seeks to maximise $\sum_{i=1}^{n} \|\mathbf{y}_i - \mathbf{y}_j\|^2$, with $\mathbf{y}_{i,j} \in \mathbf{Y}$, subject to the following constraints

$$(1) \ \|\mathbf{y}_i - \mathbf{y}_j\|^2 = \|\mathbf{x}_i - \mathbf{x}_j\|^2 \ \forall \ E(i, j) \in G$$
$$(2) \ \sum_i \bar{\mathbf{y}}_i = 0$$

where $E(i, j)$ indicates an edge in the graph G between vertex i and vertex j and so only enforces a constraint on local distances, Constraint (2) ensures the low-dimensional embedding is centred at the origin. As mentioned above, this maximisation can be reformulated as the following semidefinite programming problem.

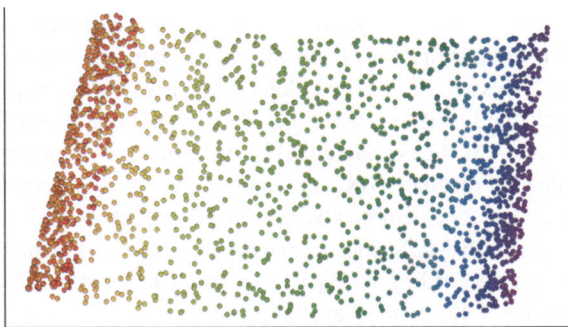

Fig. 2.5 Example
2-dimensional embeddings
of the S-Curve dataset
found by Maximum Variance
Unfolding with $k = 13$

Maximise $trace(\mathbf{F})$ subject to:

(1) $\mathbf{F} \preceq 0$.

(2) $\sum_{ij} \mathbf{f}_{ij} = 0$.

(3) $\mathbf{k}_{ii} - 2\mathbf{k}_{ij} + \mathbf{k}_{jj} = \|\mathbf{x}_i - \mathbf{x}_j\|^2 \; \forall \; E(i, j) \in G$.

Constraint (1) ensures that the matrix is positive semidefinite and Constraint (3) ensures local isometry [10].

MVU differs from other spectral techniques in that rather than constructing a feature matrix from measurable properties (i.e. covariance, Euclidean distance), it directly learns the feature matrix by solving a convex optimisation problem. Once the feature matrix has been learnt however, MVU fits in with other spectral techniques as the low-dimensional embedding is given as the top eigenvectors of Eq. (2.1).

The low-dimensional embedding of the S-Curve dataset found using MVU is shown in Fig. 2.5.

2.3.3 Diffusion Maps

The Diffusion Maps framework [11] has its roots in the field of dynamical systems. Whereas Isomap measures interpoint distances as geodesics, and MVU measures them as 'un-rolled' Euclidean distances, Diffusion Maps uses the idea of diffusion distance to capture the relationships between data points. Diffusion Maps works on a fully connected model of the data, so unlike Isomap, which considers single shortest paths, Diffusion Maps considers several paths through the data making it potentially more robust to noise. Figure 2.6 shows the 2-dimensional embedding of the S-Curve dataset founding using Diffusion Maps.

The feature matrix, $\mathbf{F}$, found by Diffusion Maps contains the diffusion distances between data points after t time steps. The diffusion distance can be found by computing a Markov random walk on a weighted graph $G = \langle V, E \rangle$, with the vertex set

Fig. 2.6 Example
2-dimensional embeddings
of the S-Curve dataset found
by Diffusion Maps with
$t = 1, \sigma = 0.1$

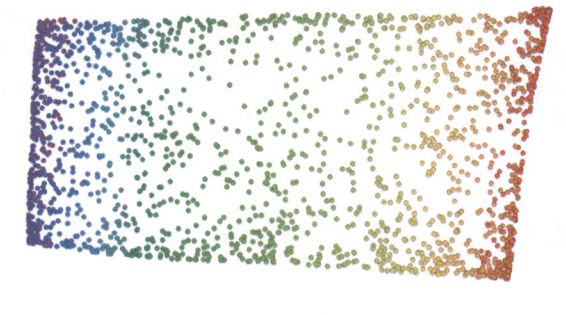

corresponding to $\mathbf{X}$ and the edge set built using the Gaussian kernel such that

$$E(i, j) = e^{-\frac{\|\mathbf{x}_i - \mathbf{x}_j\|^2}{2\sigma^2}} \tag{2.6}$$

where σ is the variance of the Gaussian. This edge set can be recast in terms of an affinity matrix such that $\mathbf{W}_{ij} = E(i, j)$, and is subsequently row normalised (the rows of $\mathbf{W}$ sum to 1) to adjust for the influence of local geometry versus distribution across the manifold [11]. The initial transition matrix $\mathbf{P}^{(1)}$ is then formed with entries $\mathbf{p}_{ij}^{(1)} = \frac{\mathbf{w}_{ij}}{d(\mathbf{x}_i)}$, where $d(\mathbf{x}_i)$ is the degree of node $\mathbf{x}_i$ such that $d(\mathbf{x}_i) = \sum_j \mathbf{w}_{ik}$. Each entry, $\mathbf{p}_{ij}^{(1)}$, can be interpreted as the forward transition probability of a diffusion process between $\mathbf{x}_i$ and $\mathbf{x}_j$ in a single timestep. The transition matrix $\mathbf{P}^{(1)}$ therefore reflects the first-order neighbourhood structure of G. Following on from this, the transition matrix $\mathbf{P}^{(t)}$ represents the probability of the diffusion process after t timesteps, and $\mathbf{p}_{ij}^{(t)}$ corresponds to the probability of going from $\mathbf{x}_i$ to $\mathbf{x}_j$ in t timesteps.

Using the forward probabilities from the random walk at timestep t, the diffusion distance between $\mathbf{x}_i$ and $\mathbf{x}_j$ can be defined by

$$\mathbf{D}^{(t)}(\mathbf{x}_i, \mathbf{x}_j) = \sum_k \frac{(\mathbf{p}_{ik}^{(t)} - \mathbf{p}_{jk}^{(t)})^2}{\phi_0(\mathbf{x}_k)} \tag{2.7}$$

where $\phi_0(\mathbf{x}_k)$ is the unique stationary distribution defined as $\frac{d(\mathbf{x}_i)}{\sum_j d(\mathbf{x}_j)}$. This term is used to assign more weight to denser regions of the graph. As can be seen from Eq. (2.7), the diffusion distance is low between data points with a high forward transition probability.

As shown in [11], the low-dimensional representation is found by the decomposition of a modified form of Eq. (2.1) such that

$$\mathbf{P}^{(t)}\mathbf{Q} = \Lambda\mathbf{Q} \tag{2.8}$$

The largest eigenvalue is trivial since the graph represented by $\mathbf{P}^{(t)}$ is fully connected, and so the associated eigenvector, $\mathbf{u}_1$, is discarded. The eigenvectors are then scaled by their eigenvalues leading to the d-dimensional embedding $\mathbf{Y} = \{\Lambda_2 \mathbf{u}_2, \Lambda_3 \mathbf{u}_3, \ldots, \Lambda_{d+1} \mathbf{u}_{d+1}\}$.

2.3.4 Locally Linear Embedding (LLE)

Although published at the same time as Isomap, LLE [12] presents a very different approach to spectral dimensionality reduction. Whereas Isomap, MVU, and Diffusion Maps, seek to construct a dense distance matrix to model global geodesic distances, LLE constructs a sparse feature matrix based on the local linear structure of the manifold. As such, LLE derives the low-dimensional embedding from the bottom eigenvectors of a sparse feature matrix and is considered a *local* technique for spectral dimensionality reduction. At a broad level, LLE works by initially describing each input data point in terms of the weights needed to reconstruct it from its nearest neighbours. These weights correspond to a description of the local geometry of each data point, and as such, the low-dimensional embedding of the data can be found by reconstructing each data point in the low-dimensional space in terms of the previously found weights. LLE is therefore a two step framework, with the weights being found in the first step by "locking" the data points, and then finding the location of the low-dimensional data points by "locking" the weights found in the first step.

The simple intuition behind LLE is that each input point, $\mathbf{x}_i$, and its k-nearest neighbours are locally linear, that is, they lie on or near a linear 'patch' of the manifold. By making this assumption the local geometry can be characterised by linear reconstruction weights, $\mathbf{W}$, that reconstruct each point $\mathbf{x}_i$ from its k-nearest neighbours. The weights are measured by the squared distance cost function

$$\varepsilon(\mathbf{W}) = \sum_i \left\| \mathbf{x}_i - \sum_j \mathbf{W}_{ij} \mathbf{x}_j \right\|^2 \tag{2.9}$$

which is minimised with the constraints: (i) $\mathbf{W}_{ij} = 0$ if $\mathbf{x}_j$ is not in the k neighbourhood of $\mathbf{x}_i$; (ii) $\sum_j \mathbf{W}_{ij} = 1$ for all i. This sparse weight matrix therefore describes the local geometry of the data up to size k. Once the weights in $\mathbf{W}$ have been found by solving the least squares problem of Eq. (2.9) using the technique described in [12], LLE seeks to reconstruct the data in the low-dimensional space by minimising the embedding cost function

$$\Phi(\mathbf{Y}) = \sum_i \left\| \mathbf{y}_i - \sum_j \mathbf{W}_{ij} \mathbf{y}_j \right\|^2 \tag{2.10}$$

Fig. 2.7 Example 2-dimensional embeddings of the S-Curve dataset found by Locally Linear Embedding with $k = 8$

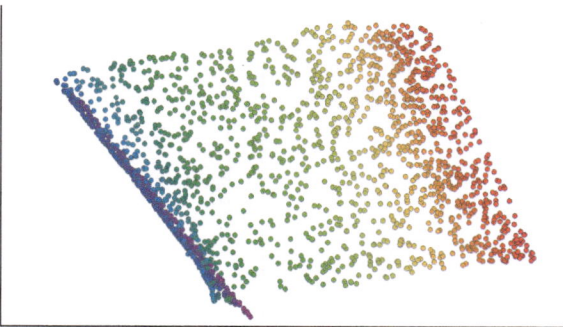

with the specific constraints: (i) $\sum_i \mathbf{y}_i = 0$, that is, the outputs are centered; (ii) the outputs have unit covariance. These constraints prevent a degenerate solution and also allow the minimisation of Eq. (2.10) to be found through the computation of the bottom $(d + 1)$ eigenvectors of the feature matrix $\mathbf{F} = (\mathbf{I} - \mathbf{W})^T (\mathbf{I} - \mathbf{W})$, where the bottom eigenvector (corresponding to the constant unit vector) is discarded.

Figure 2.7 shows the 2-dimensional embedding of the S-Curve dataset found using LLE. As can be seen, since LLE is a local approach to dimensionality reduction, the global shape of the manifold is not fully recovered.

Although similar methods existed before LLE to model the local geometry of a manifold (e.g. Local PCA [13]), the novel feature of LLE is that it maps the local geometric models into a single, coherent, coordinate system. As well as this, by modelling the local geometry in terms of reconstruction coefficients, the core methodology of LLE can be used to embed new data points into a previously learnt manifold, a problem which is described in more detail in Chap. 5.

2.3.5 Laplacian Eigenmaps

Similar to LLE, Laplacian Eigenmaps [14] seeks to find a low-dimensional embedding through the preservation of local neighbourhood properties. As in LLE, a weight matrix is employed to capture the local structure of the data, and the low-dimensional embedding is found through the bottom $(d + 1)$ eigenvectors of this sparse feature matrix. While LLE appeals to geometric intuition to model the local properties of the data, Laplacian Eigenmaps appeals to spectral graph theory and the notion of the graph Laplacian to find a solution to the minimisation of the central cost function.

Laplacian Eigenmaps seeks to minimise the following embedding cost function:

$$\Phi(\mathbf{Y}) = \sum_{ij} (\mathbf{y}_i - \mathbf{y}_j)^2 \mathbf{w}_{ij} \tag{2.11}$$

Fig. 2.8 Example 2-
dimensional embeddings
of the S-Curve dataset found
by Laplacian Eigenmaps with
$k = 12, \sigma = 2$

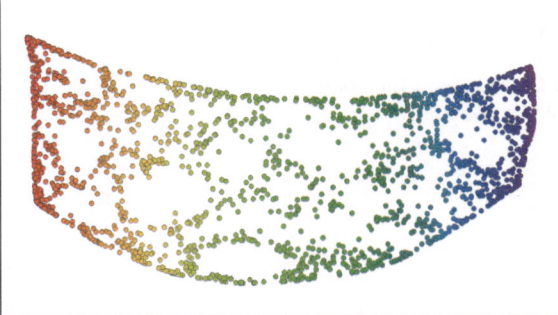

where large weights in $\mathbf{W}$ correspond to small distances in the high-dimensional space and so nearby points in $\mathbf{X}$ are brought together in $\mathbf{Y}$ with 'nearness' being represented by the weight values in $\mathbf{W}$. The weight matrix can be constructed in numerous ways with the most common forms being either to assign constant weights, $\mathbf{w}_{ij} = 1/k$, or to use a heat kernel to exponentially decay the weights, $\mathbf{w}_{ij} = \exp(-\|\mathbf{x}_i - \mathbf{x}_j\|^2)/\sigma^2$ where σ is a scale parameter defining the size of the kernel.

As shown in [14], the solution to Eq. (2.11) can be found by recasting it in terms of a general eigenproblem involving the Laplacian of the graph. The Laplacian matrix, $\mathbf{F}$, is defined as $\mathbf{F} = \mathbf{M} - \mathbf{W}$ where $\mathbf{M}$ is the degree matrix of $\mathbf{W}$ such that $\mathbf{m}_{ij} = \sum_j \mathbf{w}_{ij}$. With this in mind, the cost function of Eq. (2.11) can be re-formulated as

$$
\begin{aligned}
\Phi(\mathbf{Y}) &= \sum_{ij} (\mathbf{y}_i - \mathbf{y}_j)^2 \mathbf{w}_{ij} \\
&= \sum_{ij} (\mathbf{y}_i^2 + \mathbf{y}_j^2 - 2\mathbf{y}_i\mathbf{y}_j) \mathbf{w}_{ij} \\
&= \sum_i \mathbf{y}_i^2 \mathbf{D}_{ii} + \sum_j \mathbf{y}_j^2 \mathbf{D}_{jj} - 2 \sum_{ij} \mathbf{y}_i\mathbf{y}_j \mathbf{w}_{ij} \\
&= 2\mathbf{Y}^T \mathbf{F} \mathbf{Y}
\end{aligned}
\tag{2.12}
$$

Therefore, the minimisation of Eq. (2.11) can be found by observing that $\mathbf{F}$ is positive semidefinite, and so the values of $\mathbf{Y}$ that minimise the objective function are given by the solution to the eigenvalue problem $\mathbf{F}\mathbf{Y} = \Lambda\mathbf{D}\mathbf{Y}$. As with LLE, the bottom (smallest) eigenvector is discarded and the $(d + 1)$ smallest eigenvectors give rise to the q-dimensional embedding. Figure 2.8 shows the low-dimensional embedding of the S-Curve dataset found using Laplacian Eigenmaps.

One further point of interest with regards to Laplacian Eigenmaps is the algorithm's linearised variant, Locality Preserving Projections (LPP) [15]. LPP seeks to compute a transformation matrix using the graph Laplacian that maps the data points into a subspace. Specifically, LPP seeks to minimise

$$\underset{\substack{\mathbf{a} \\ \mathbf{a}^T \mathbf{XDX}^T \mathbf{a} = 1}}{\arg\min} \quad \mathbf{a}^T \mathbf{XDX}^T \mathbf{a} \tag{2.13}$$

where $\mathbf{a}$ is a transformation vector. The vectors, $\mathbf{a}$, that minimise the above objective function are given by the smallest eigenvectors of the generalised eigenproblem $\mathbf{XFX}^T \mathbf{a} = \lambda \mathbf{XDX}^T \mathbf{a}$. Locality Preserving Projections has proved useful in many problem domains due to its linearity and speed, and also due to the fact that it naturally incorporates the mapping of new points. This is discussed in more detail in Chap. 5.

2.3.6 Local Tangent Space Alignment (LTSA)

The Local Tangent Space Alignment method [16] models the data in terms of the local tangent space of each data point. The tangent space for a data point can conceptually be thought of as an approximation of the principal manifold at a local scale passing through the data point. The tangent spaces for a set of near neighbours are assumed to be overlapping, and so the global co-ordinate system can be found by aligning the local tangent spaces. LTSA therefore builds a global representation of the data by aligning a set of local models.

The local information for a data point $\mathbf{x}_i$ is calculated by finding the q largest eignvectors of the correction matrix $\mathbf{W}_i$ of the neighbourhood around $\mathbf{x}_i$ such that

$$\mathbf{W}_i = (\mathbf{X}_{\mathcal{N}_i} - \bar{\mathbf{x}}_i \mathbf{e}^T)^T (\mathbf{X}_{\mathcal{N}_i} - \bar{\mathbf{x}}_i \mathbf{e}^T) \tag{2.14}$$

where $\mathbf{X}_{\mathcal{N}_i}$ corresponds to the points in $\mathbf{X}$ that appear in the k-neighbourhood of $\mathbf{x}_i$ represented as $\mathcal{N}_i$ and $\mathbf{e}$ is a k-dimensional column vector of ones. The local information, $\mathbf{G}_i$, is then built from the largest eignvectors of $\mathbf{W}_i$ such that $\mathbf{G}_i = [\mathbf{e}/\sqrt{k}, \mathbf{g}_1, \mathbf{g}_2, \ldots, \mathbf{g}_q]$ where $\mathbf{e}/\sqrt{k}$ is a centering term.

LTSA seeks to minimise a cost function that minimises the distances between points in the low-dimensional space and the tangent space. As shown in [16], the solution to this minimisation problem is formed by the d smallest eigenvectors of an alignment matrix $\mathbf{F}$. The alignment matrix is found by iteratively summing over all local information matrices:

$$\mathbf{F}_{\mathcal{N}_i, \mathcal{N}_i} \leftarrow \mathbf{F}_{\mathcal{N}_i, \mathcal{N}_i} + \mathbf{H}_k (\mathbf{I} - \mathbf{G}_i \mathbf{G}_i^T) \mathbf{H}_k \tag{2.15}$$

starting from $\mathbf{F} = 0$ for $\forall i j$. Here, $\mathbf{H}_k$ is a centering matrix of size k with $\mathbf{H}_k = \mathbf{I}_k - \frac{1}{k}\mathbf{e}\mathbf{e}^T$ where e is a k-dimensional column vector of all ones.

The low-dimensional representation $\mathbf{Y}$ is given by the bottom $(d+1)$ eigenvectors of $\mathbf{F}$ found according to Eq. (2.1) with the smallest eigenvector being discarded. An example low-dimensional embedding of the S-Curve dataset found using Local Tangent Space Alignment is given in Fig. 2.9.

Fig. 2.9 Example
2-dimensional embeddings
of the S-Curve dataset found
by Local Tangent Space
Alignment with $k = 10$

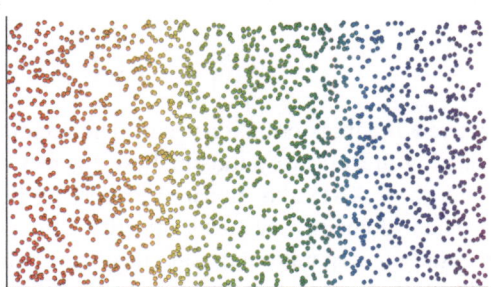

Table 2.1 The kernel form of each technique is described relative to each specific feature matrix **F**

Method	Properties	Kernel form
Linear [1, 4]	Top eigenvectors	$\mathbf{K} = \kappa(\mathbf{x}_i, \mathbf{x}_j)$ where κ is an appropriately chosen kernel function
Isomap [2]	Top eigenvectors	$\mathbf{K} = -\frac{1}{2}\mathbf{H}\tau(\mathbf{S})\mathbf{H}$ where $\tau(\mathbf{S})$ is the squared distance matrix and **H** is the centering matrix
MVU [8]	Top eigenvectors	As given (Sect. 2.3.2)
Diffusion maps [11]	Top eigenvectors	As given (Sect. 2.3.3)
LLE [12]	Bottom eigenvectors	$\mathbf{K} = \mathbf{H}(\lambda_{\max}\mathbf{I} - \mathbf{F})\mathbf{H}$ where $\lambda_{\max}$ is the maximum eigenvalue of **F**
Eigenmaps [14]	Bottom eigenvectors	$\mathbf{K} = \mathbf{H}\mathbf{F}^{\dagger}\mathbf{H}$ where $\mathbf{F}^{\dagger}$ is the pseudo-inverse of the Laplacian matrix
LTSA [16]	Bottom eigenvectors	$\mathbf{K} = \mathbf{I} - \mathbf{F}$

For a definition of **F** with respect to each technique see Sects. 2.2.1–2.3.6

2.4 Kernel Formulation

There have been numerous attempts to phrase spectral dimensionality reduction
within a unified framework, examples being Graph Embedding [17], and a unified
probabilistic framework [18]. But perhaps one of the most significant and useful unified settings is found when phrasing spectral dimensionality reduction algorithms as
kernel methods [19]. All spectral methods can be described as performing Kernel
Principal Components Analysis [20] on specially constructed Gram matrices (e.g.
Kernel Isomap, LLE, and Laplacian Eigenmaps [19], Kernel LTSA [21]). It is worth
noting that Maximum Variance Unfolding [8] and Diffusion Maps [11] already construct kernel matrices so they do not need to be adapted to fit within this framework.
Table 2.1 summarises the kernel form of each of the discussed spectral dimensionality reduction algorithms. These kernel forms will be useful in later chapters when
solutions from the kernel methods community can be applied to kernel based spectral
dimensionality reduction techniques.

2.5 Summary

Spectral dimensionality reduction seeks to obtain a low-dimensional embedding of a high-dimensional dataset through the eigendecomposition of a specially constructed feature matrix. This feature matrix will capture certain properties of the data such as inter-point covariance or local linear reconstruction weights. The different methods of formulating this feature matrix will have different implications for various open problems, as will be seen in later chapters.

References

1. Joliffe, I.T.: Principal Component Analysis. Springer-Verlag, New York (1986)
2. Tenenbaum, J.B., de Silva, V., Langford, J.C.: A global geometric framework for nonlinear dimensionality reduction. Science **290**, 2319–2322 (2000)
3. Hotelling, H.: Analysis of a complex of statistical variables into principal components. Journal of Educational Psychology **24**, 417–441 (1933)
4. Cox, T.F., Cox, M.A.A.: Multidimensional Scaling. Chapman and Hall (2001)
5. Saul, L.K., Weinberger, K.Q., Ham, J.H., Sha, F., Lee, D.D.: Semisupervised Learning, chap. Spectral Methods for Dimensionality Reduction, pp. 293–308. MIT Press, Cambridge, MA (2006)
6. Rowlinson, P.: Graph Connections: Relationships Between Graph Theory and other Areas of Mathematics, chap. Linear Algebra, pp. 86–99. Oxford Science Publications (1997)
7. Dijkstra, E.W.: A note on two problems in connexion with graphs. Numerische Mathematik **1**, 269–271 (1959)
8. Weinberger, K.Q., Packer, B.D., Saul, L.K.: Nonlinear dimensionality reduction by semidefinite programming and kernel matrix factorization. In: In Proceedings of the Tenth International Workshop on Artificial Intelligence and Statistics, pp. 381–388 (2005)
9. Vandenberghe, L., Boyd, S.P.: Semidefinite programming. SIAM Review **38**(1), 49–95 (1996)
10. Weinberger, K.Q., Sha, F., Saul, L.K.: Learning a kernel matrix for nonlinear dimensionality reduction. In: In Proceedings of the 21st International Conference on Machine Learning, pp. 839–846 (2004)
11. Lafon, S., Lee, A.B.: Diffusion maps and coarse-graining: A unified framework for dimensionality reduction, graph partitioning, and data set parameterization. IEEE Transactions on Pattern Analysis and Machine Intelligence **28**(9), 1393–1403 (2006)
12. Roweis, S.T., Saul, L.K.: Nonlinear dimensionality reduction by Locally Linear Embedding. Science **290**, 2323–2326 (2000)
13. Kambhatla, N., Leen, T.K.: Dimension reduction by local Principal Components Analysis. Neural Computation **9**(7), 1493–1516 (1994)
14. Belkin, M., Niyogi, P.: Laplacian eigenmaps and spectral techniques for embedding and clustering. In: Advances in Neural Information Processing Systems 14: Proceedings of the 2002 Conference (NIPS), pp. 585–591 (2002)
15. He, X., Niyogi, P.: Locality Preserving Projections. In: Advances in Neural Information Processing Systems 16: Proceedings of the 2003 Conference (NIPS), pp. 153–160. MIT Press (2003)
16. Zhang, Z., Zha, H.: Principal manifolds and nonlinear dimension reduction via local tangent space alignment. SIAM Journal on Scientific Computing **26**(1), 313–338 (2004)
17. Yan, S., Xu, D., Zhang, B., Zhang, H.J., Yang, Q., Lin, S.: Graph embedding: A general framework for dimensionality reduction. IEEE Transactions on Pattern Analysis and Machine Intelligence **29**(1), 40–51 (2007)

18. Lawrence, N.D.: A unifying probabilistic perspective for spectral dimensionality reduction: Insights and new models. Journal of Machine Learning Research **13**, 1609–1638 (2012)
19. Ham, J., Lee, D.D., Mika, S., Schölkopf, B.: A kernel view of the dimensionality reduction of manifolds. In: In Proceedings of the 21st International Conference on Machine Learning, pp. 47–55 (2004)
20. Scholkopf, B., Smola, E., Bottou, L., Burges, C., Bultho, H., Gegenfurtner, K., Ner, P.H.: Nonlinear component analysis as a kernel eigenvalue problem. Neural Computation **10**, 1299–1319 (1998)
21. Ma, L., Crawford, M.M., Tian, J.W.: Generalised supervised local tangent space alignment for hyperspectral image classification. Electronics Letters **46**(7), 497–498 (2010)

Chapter 3
Modelling the Manifold

Abstract In this chapter, an overview of some of the key issues associated with modelling manifolds are provided. This covers the construction of neighbourhood graphs, and automatic estimation of relevant parameters; how manifold modelling techniques deal with various topologies of the data; and the problem of noise. Each of these aspects are supported by an illustrative example. The interaction between these key issues is also discussed.

Keywords Neighbourhood graphs · Manifold approximations · Noise and outliers · Data topologies

For nonlinear spectral dimensionality reduction methods a neighbourhood graph is induced over the dataset that attempts to approximate the connectivity and structure of the underlying manifold. The construction of such a graph is however a non-trivial process. Although using a nearest neighbour graph has been proven effective, there are still issues that need to be addressed with regard to the parameters used to construct the graph. As well as this, there are certain situations which spectral dimensionality reduction does not handle well, such as multiple manifolds and noisy data. These problems all combine into the single problem of how the manifold be can be adequately modelled.

This chapter seeks to overview these manifold modelling problems and is split into three sections: the first deals with the problem of constructing a neighbourhood graph that accurately models the underlying manifold. The second section outlines the problems associated with manifolds that contain difficult topologies and multiple sub-manifolds. The third section details approaches that can be used to help overcome the problem of noise. One of the key issues with modelling the manifold is that these three sections cannot be thought of independently. There will be overlap and interplay between the problems from each section, a point that is raised and discussed in the summary of this chapter.

H. Strange and R. Zwiggelaar, *Open Problems in Spectral Dimensionality Reduction*,   23
SpringerBriefs in Computer Science, DOI: 10.1007/978-3-319-03943-5_3,
© The Author(s) 2014

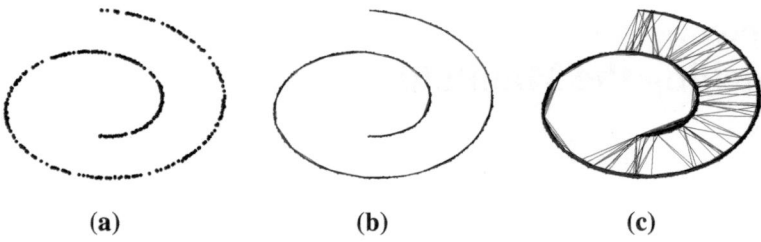

(a)   **(b)**   **(c)**

Fig. 3.1 A set of points are sampled from a 1-dimensional manifold 'curled up' on itself in 2-dimensional space **a**. A good approximation of the neighbourhood graph is shown in **b** where there are no gaps in the graph and no jumps that short-circuit the manifold. (**c**) shows an example of where the neighbourhood graph is inadequately estimated; there are multiple short-circuits where points are joined as neighbours but do not lie on the same patch of the manifold

3.1 Overview of Neighbourhood Graph Construction

All nonlinear spectral dimensionality reduction techniques model the inter-point relationships through the use of a neighbourhood graph. That is not to say that all techniques leverage the same relationships from this graph; for example, Isomap [1] will extract the global geodesic distances whilst Laplacian Eigenmaps [2] utilises the graph Laplacian. Both lead to different embeddings yet both are built from the same initial building block—a neighbourhood graph. Although these techniques all utilise a neighbourhood graph, the method used to construct the graph is left as an open problem.

The basic premise of neighbourhood graph construction is to 'connect' points that lie within a common neighbourhood. This neighbourhood can be defined in many ways; traditionally, the two ways that a neighbourhood can be defined is either using the *k-nearest neighbour approach*—defining a neighbourhood as the k points that lie closest to the given point according to a distance metric—or the *ε-neighbourhood approach*—connecting points that lie within a radius of size ε around a given point. Both methods rely on the careful choice of parameter, either k or ε, and the choice of value for the parameter can have far reaching consequences. If the value is too small, that is the neighbourhood is *under approximated*, then the neighbourhood graph may not be fully connected, that is, there may be small clusters of neighbourhoods that do not join together. As well as this, if the neighbourhood is under approximated then there may be insufficient information to reconstruct the local geometry of the manifold. Conversely, if the neighbourhood size value is too large, that is the neighbourhood is *over approximated*, then the neighbourhood graph may become short-circuited. A short-circuit can be thought of as two points being connected on the graph when they do not lie on the same 'patch' of manifold (See Fig. 3.1). Also, if the neighbourhood is over approximated then the local linear assumption may be broken as the neighbourhood may span more than a single 'patch' of the manifold.

The problem of choosing a neighbourhood size value, be it k or ε, is an interesting one that has received much attention in the literature due to its importance. One of the inherent problems is that in a real world setting it is difficult to assess whether a neighbourhood value k_1 is *better* than another value k_2. A naïve approach may be to produce two embeddings, one using k_1 and one using k_2, and then assess which one is better or more suitable. There are numerous problems with such a simplistic approach; for example, in a real world setting, what constitutes a better embedding? This is something that is touched upon in Chap. 7 but assessing the quality of an embedding can itself be an open problem. As well as this, what is to say that it is either k_1 or k_2 that provides a suitable embedding? It could be the case that both values are unsuitable and so a range of values may need to be tested. If the dataset is large then testing the embedding over a range of different neighbourhood sizes could be unrealistic as it will take time to compute each embedding.

What should be readily apparent is that choosing a neighbourhood size value is a more involved process than simply testing a range of values and seeing which one is "the best". Rather, techniques have been proposed that allow the neighbourhood size value to be automatically estimated for a given dataset so that the data itself can be used to define an appropriate neighbourhood size value.

3.2 Building Neighbourhood Graphs

Before examining the various methods developed to automatically select a value for k, it is worth recalling how a k-neighbourhood graph is constructed. Given a dataset $\mathbf{X} \in \mathbb{R}^D$ a graph $G = \langle V, E \rangle$ is sought such that V is the vertex set containing a single vertex for each element of $\mathbf{X}$, and E is the edge set. Since V is given, the goal is to find the edge set according to the following rule: an edge $e_{ij} \in E$ is created for each pair of vertices v_i and v_j if they are part of the set of k-nearest neighbours, that is $v_j \in \mathcal{N}_i$. Here, $\mathcal{N}_i$ denotes the set of k-nearest neighbour vertices for v_i which can be found using any standard nearest neighbour search algorithm [3–5].

The simplest approaches to neighbourhood size selection are those that work with a specific spectral dimensionality reduction method (i.e. they are not generalisable). One such technique for Isomap [6] bears much resemblance to the naïve approach discussed above. The basic premise of the technique proposed in [6] is to estimate a range of k values, K, with $k_{\min} \in K$ corresponding to the smaller value for which the neighbourhood graph is connected, and $k_{\max} \in K$ being the largest value in the equation:

$$\frac{2|E|}{n} \ll k + 2 \tag{3.1}$$

where $|E|$ is the total number of edges in G. The optimal value, k_{opt} is then assumed to lie within these two values, that is $k_{\text{opt}} \in [k_{\min}, k_{\max}] = K$. The optimal value for k is then found by estimating the embedding error of Isomap for all values within K are determining the value which minimises

$$k_{\text{opt}} = \arg\min_{k}(1 - \rho^2_{\mathbf{D_X},\mathbf{D_Y}}) \tag{3.2}$$

where ρ is the linear correlation coefficient and $\mathbf{D_X}$ and $\mathbf{D_Y}$ are the matrices of Euclidean distances in the high and low dimensional spaces, respectively. As such, the optimal value of k is assumed to be the one which minimises the central cost function of the Isomap algorithm [1, 6]. It is worth noting that this algorithm can also be used to determine the optimal ε neighbours as well by simply replacing the k nearest neighbour criteria with the ε neighbour rule.

A similar method to that described above but applied to LLE [7] was presented in [8]. Two algorithms were presented, both of which are based on the optimal value equation shown in Eq. 3.2. The most straightforward method follows the same approach as that outlined above, however, the second, hierarchical, method differs slightly. The local reconstruction error, ε, of LLE (Eq. 2.9) can be thought of as a function of k, with a smaller value of ε corresponding to a better approximation of the local linear structure of the manifold. As such, the optimal value, k_{opt}, can correspond to the smallest value of ε [8]. Therefore, ε is computed over a range of k values, $k \in [1, k_{\text{max}}]$. Since LLE does not guarantee a single minimum, there may be multiple potential candidates, S, for the optimal value of k. The residual variance is then computed over the set of potential candidates S to obtain a final optimal value for k.

Although results show that both methods can find an "optimal" value of k for Isomap and LLE they do both require the spectral dimensionality reduction techniques to be run multiple times over the range of parameters, a potentially costly procedure (as discussed in Chap. 6). As well as this, it is assumed that the residual variance is a good measure of the optimality of an embedding. This may of course not always be the case and so both techniques are not so much techniques for finding the optimal parameter values for Isomap and LLE, but rather they are techniques that find the optimal parameter values to minimise the residual variance.

3.2.1 Optimised Neighbourhood Methods

In the case where there is no technique specific k-neighbourhood estimation method, a generalised estimation algorithm is required. These generalised methods are independent of the spectral dimensionality reduction method used and interrogate the data to attempt to build a robust neighbourhood graph based on a given value of k. Two such approaches which have proven effective for building a k-nearest neighbour graph independently of any dimensionality reduction method are the k-edge disjoint spanning tree algorithm [9] and the graph algebra algorithm [10]. Although these methods do not estimate an optimal value of k, they do attempt to build a graph that is fully connected and has optimised neighbourhoods for the given k value.

The goal of the k-edge disjoint spanning tree algorithm (Min-k-ST) [9] is to find a neighbourhood graph, $G = \langle V, E \rangle$, that is minimally k-edge connected.

A graph is considered k-edge connected if it remains connected whenever fewer than k edges are removed. A graph is considered minimally k-edge connected if, for every edge $e \in E$, the graph $\langle V, E - \{e\} \rangle$ is not k-edge connected. The Min-k-ST algorithm builds a set of k-edge disjoint spanning trees whose total edge length is guaranteed to be minimum and the final neighbourhood graph is constructed by combining the set of k-edge disjoint spanning trees. To achieve this, a modified form of Kruskal's algorithm [11] for minimum spanning tree (MST) construction is used. Kruskal's algorithm initially partitions the vertex set V into a forest of n trees, that is, each tree in Kruskal's initial forest consists of one vertex. Each edge is then processed in nondecreasing order of length and, if an edge connects two different trees in the forest, then the edge is added and the two trees are merged. This continues until only a single tree remains. The modified version of Kruskal's algorithm works by maintaining k edge-disjoint forests as opposed to a single forest. One of the fundamental concepts of the modified algorithm is that of a k-edge-connected component (referred to hereon as a component) which corresponds to a tree that is well established to span a common set of vertices [9]. Whenever an edge is added the forests are updated, if both ends of an incoming edge are in a component then the edge is dropped. If an incoming edge connects two components the edge is added and the two components are merged. The Min-k-ST algorithm stops when all vertices belong to a single component. Although the Min-k-ST algorithm does guarantee the neighbourhood graph to be k-edge connected, it comes at a potentially high computational cost. Kruskal's algorithm uses a heap sort data structure which has a memory requirement of $O(|E|)$ which restricts the use of Min-k-ST to small datasets only.

The graph algebra method [10] for optimised neighbourhood graph building seeks to employ techniques from path algebra [12, 13] to build the neighbourhood graph. One of the central concepts of path algebra is that two objects can be considered as similar if they are connected by a chain of intermediate objects whose dissimilarities or distances are small. As such, the graph algebra method for neighbourhood graph construction seeks to assign two data points as neighbours if they can be connected by a mediating path of intermediate points [10]. The graph algebra algorithm begins by constructing a standard k-nearest neighbour graph using an initial choice of k, and then examines each data point in turn and seeks to optimise that neighbourhood. The set of k nearest neighbours of each point, $\mathcal{N}_i$, are examined and for each point in $\mathcal{N}_i$ the m-nearest neighbours, denoted $\mathcal{M}_{\mathcal{N}_i}$, are examined (with $m \leq k$). As such, the graph algebra algorithm can be thought of as examining the nearest neighbours of the nearest neighbours. The neighbourhood optimisation takes the form of replacing large connections within the initial neighbourhood $\mathcal{N}_i$ with any smaller connections found in $\mathcal{M}_{\mathcal{N}_i}$.

Although the proposed graph algebra approach does present good results with a small computational overhead, there are no guarantees that a k-edge connected graph is formed. As such, it may be that an initial choice of k may be too small to produce a fully connected graph.

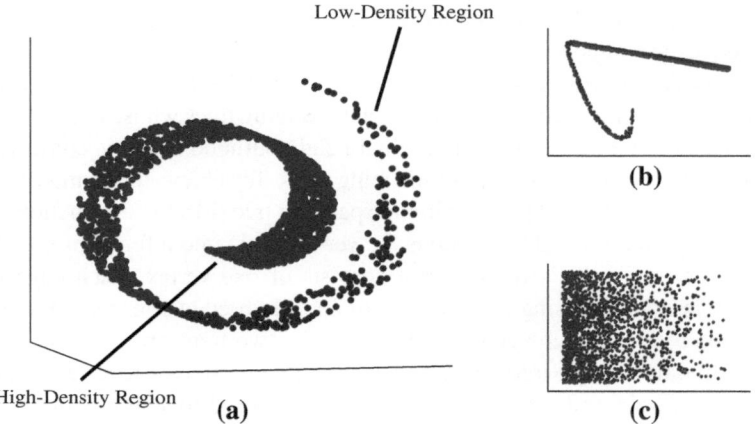

Fig. 3.2 An example of the Swiss Roll dataset with changing data density (**a**). When using a single k value (**b**), the low-dimensional embedding becomes highly distorted. However, if an adaptive neighbourhood estimation technique is used (**c**), then the low-dimensional embedding can be correctly recovered as different values of k are assigned for the different density regions

3.2.2 Adaptive Estimation Methods

Adaptive neighbourhood estimation methods seek to move away from the rigid assumption that a single value of k is sufficient to model the manifold structure of the data. One of the assumptions of all of the previously described methods for neighbourhood selection and building is that the manifold can be adequately modelled at every data point by a single k value. This assumes that the data is sampled in such a way that at all points on the manifold can be locally approximated by k-nearest neighbours. An example of where this may not be the case is shown in Fig. 3.2. To overcome this problem, adaptive neighbourhood estimation methods seek to adapt the neighbourhood to "fit" the data. Interestingly, all the adaptive methods described below seek to exploit the tangent spaces around each datapoint to derive a neighbourhood graph.

Unsurprisingly, the adaptive neighbourhood estimation methods that utilise the local tangent spaces are firmly grounded within the framework of Local Tangent Space Alignment (LTSA) [14]. In fact, the initial adaptive neighbourhood selection was presented as an improved form of LTSA referred to as adaptive manifold learning (AML) [15, 16]. AML adaptively selects a value k_i at each data point $\mathbf{x}_i$ through a contraction and expansion algorithm. The contraction step seeks to move from an over approximated neighbourhood to one that compactly represents the local neighbourhood of $\mathbf{x}_i$, while the expansion step simply adds data points back to a neighbourhood so that overlap between neighbourhoods is improved. The contraction algorithm has five steps detailed below:

1. Given an initial estimate of k, the k-nearest neighbours of each data point in $\mathbf{X}$ are stored such that $\mathcal{N}_i^{(k)} = \{\mathbf{x}_{i1}, \mathbf{x}_{i2}, \dots, \mathbf{x}_{ik}\}$ represents the set of k neighbours of $\mathbf{x}_i$ ordered in non-decreasing distance to $\mathbf{x}_i$. Set $j = k$.

2. The mean of $\mathcal{N}_i^{(j)}$ is denoted $\bar{\mathbf{x}}_i^{(j)}$. The orthogonal basis matrix $\mathbf{Q}_i^j$ and the d largest singular vectors of $(\mathcal{N}_i^{(j)} - \bar{\mathbf{x}}_i^{(j)}\mathbf{e}^T)$ are then computed. The projection onto the local tangent space is then computed as $\Theta_i^{(j)} = (\mathbf{Q}_i^{(j)})^T(\mathcal{N}_i^{(j)} - \bar{\mathbf{x}}_i^{(j)}\mathbf{e}^T)$.

3. If $||\mathcal{N}_i^{(j)} - \bar{\mathbf{x}}_i^{(j)}\mathbf{e}^T - \mathbf{Q}_i^{(j)}\Theta_i^{(j)}||_F < \eta||\Theta_i^{(j)}||$ then set $\mathcal{N}_i = \mathcal{N}_i^{(j)}$ and terminate. Here, $||\cdot||_F$ corresponds to the Frobenius norm.

4. Otherwise, if $k > (d + k_0)$ for some small k_0, then remove the last nearest neighbour from $\mathcal{N}_i^{(j)}$ (i.e. the furthest from $\mathbf{x}_i$) to obtain $\mathcal{N}_i^{(j-1)}$, set $j := j - 1$ and go to step 2, otherwise continue to step 5.

5. Let $j = \arg\min_{d+k_0 \leq p \leq k} \dfrac{||\mathcal{N}_i^{(p)} - \bar{\mathbf{x}}_i^{(p)}\mathbf{e}^T - \mathbf{Q}_i^{(p)}\Theta_i^{(p)}||_F}{||\Theta_i^{(p)}||_F}$, and set $\mathcal{N}_i = \mathcal{N}_i^j$.

The neighbourhood contraction algorithm is conceptually very simple: starting with a large value of k, the tangent space is constructed and the criteria for neighbourhood selection $||\mathcal{N}_i^{(j)} - \bar{\mathbf{x}}_i^{(j)}\mathbf{e}^T - \mathbf{Q}_i^{(j)}\Theta_i^{(j)}||_F < \eta||\Theta_i^{(j)}||$ is checked. If the criteria is met then the neighbourhood contraction has completed, otherwise the neighbourhood is made smaller by removing the point in $\mathcal{N}_i$ that is furthest away from $\mathbf{x}_i$ and the process is repeated. The final step ensures that there is a solution to the neighbourhood selection problem even if no value satisfies the above criteria. Once the neighbourhoods have been contracted to their most compact form, they are subsequently expanded to ensure that there is sufficient overlap between them (an important step when using the adaptive neighbourhood method for LTSA). The expansion method works by taking the neighbourhood found during contraction, $\mathcal{N}_i$, and assigning j_i to be the number of neighbours in $\mathcal{N}_i$. For $p = j_i + 1, \dots, k$, compute $\theta_p^{(i)} = \mathbf{Q}_i^T(\mathbf{x}_{i_p} - \bar{\mathbf{x}}_i)$. Let P_i denote the index subset of p's, $j_i < p \leq k$, such that $||(\mathbf{I} - \mathbf{Q}_i\mathbf{Q}_i^T)(\mathbf{x}_{i_p} - \bar{\mathbf{X}}_i||^2 \leq ||\theta_p^{(i)}||^2$. Expand $\mathcal{N}_i$ by adding $\mathbf{x}_{i_p}$, $p \in P_i$.

Although AML gives much improved results over standard k-neighbourhood graph formation methods, it still requires an initial guess parameter for k and also a user defined threshold η used to compare the ratio of Frobenius norms. As well as this, the adaptive neighbourhood method will show less significant improvements when the underlying geometry of the manifold complex, that is, if the geometry is difficult to determine from a small set of data points [16].

One similar method to AML is parameterless Isomap [17] that seeks to improve upon AML by removing the user defined threshold parameter η. Parameterless Isomap is not restricted to the Isomap algorithm, and unlike AML, parameterless Isomap builds the neighbourhood around each point by expanding a neighbourhood as opposed to contracting it. The neighbourhood around a point $\mathbf{x}_i$ is grown one point at a time until the following criteria is violated when adding a new point $\mathbf{x}_{ij}$ to the neighbourhood:

$$||(\mathbf{I} - \mathbf{Q}_i\mathbf{Q}_i^T)(\mathbf{x}_{ij} - \mathbf{x}_i)||^2 < \tilde{T}_1(\mathbf{x}_i) \tag{3.3}$$

where, $\tilde{T}_1(\mathbf{x}_i)$ represents the estimated radius of the neighbourhood such that $\tilde{T}_1(\mathbf{x}_i) = (1/k)^{(1/d)}||\mathbf{x}_{ik} - \mathbf{x}_i||^2$. The key advantages of parameterless Isomap is that it requires no parameters for the neighbourhood graph construction, as well as this, it may add an unlimited number of neighbours as long as the linear tangent space assumption is upheld [17]. One of the main drawbacks of the parameterless Isomap approach is that for large datasets the condition given in Eq. 3.3 can not always be satisfied and so the neighbourhood can not be determined [18]. With this in mind, another approach was presented, dynamical neighbourhood selection [18], to adaptively select the neighbourhood around a datapoint that follows a similar approach to AML and parameterless Isomap but uses the manifold density and curvature to help determine values of k.

The dynamical neighbourhood selection algorithm works on very similar principles to that of AML and parameterless Isomap, however, it differs by examining the deviation of angles of neighbouring points to a target points tangent subspace. If the angle of a point $\mathbf{x}_j$ to the tangent subspace of a point $\mathbf{x}_i$ is smaller than a value $\tilde{\theta}$ then $\mathbf{x}_j$ is considered a neighbour of $\mathbf{x}_i$. As well as this, the dynamical neighbourhood selection algorithm seeks to provide a more robust definition of the neighbourhood radius, $\tilde{T}_1(\mathbf{x}_i)$ by introducing a relaxation parameter ζ such that

$$\tilde{T}_1(\mathbf{x}_i) = \zeta \min \left\{ (1/k)^{(1/d)}||\mathbf{x}_k^{(i)} - \mathbf{x}_i||^2, ||\mathbf{x}_1^{(i)} - \mathbf{x}_i||^2 \right\} \tag{3.4}$$

where $||\mathbf{x}_1^{(i)} - \mathbf{x}_i||^2$ is the Euclidean distance between $\mathbf{x}_i$ and its nearest neighbour. The relaxation parameter, ζ has the range $(0, 1]$ and its optimal value can be estimated through the residual variance between points in the input and output space: $\zeta_{opt} = \arg\min_\zeta (1 - \rho^2_{\mathbf{G},\mathbf{D_Y}})$. Here, $\mathbf{G}$ corresponds to the geodesic distances measured in the high-dimensional space and $\mathbf{D_Y}$ corresponds to the Euclidean distances in the low-dimensional space.

The neighbourhood around a point $\mathbf{x}_i$ is then iteratively built by adding another point $\mathbf{x}_j$ if and only if $\theta_j < \tilde{\theta}$ and $||(\mathbf{I} - \mathbf{Q}_i\mathbf{Q}_i^T)(\mathbf{x}_{ij} - \mathbf{x}_i)||^2 < \tilde{T}_1(\mathbf{x}_i)$. Although this method may overcome some of the shortcomings of the parameterless Isomap method, it is not without its own problems. For example, it relies on an angle threshold, $\tilde{\theta}$ that must be supplied, as well as a relaxation factor, ζ, that, although can be computed automatically, comes at an extra computational cost.

3.3 Topological and Multi-manifold Considerations

Sometimes the data under consideration will be sampled from a manifold that may contain a complex topology or multiple 'parts' and as such existing strategies for modelling such manifolds will fail to give optimal results. Special consideration has been given in the literature to each of these areas as they present not only interesting research problems, but also important solutions.

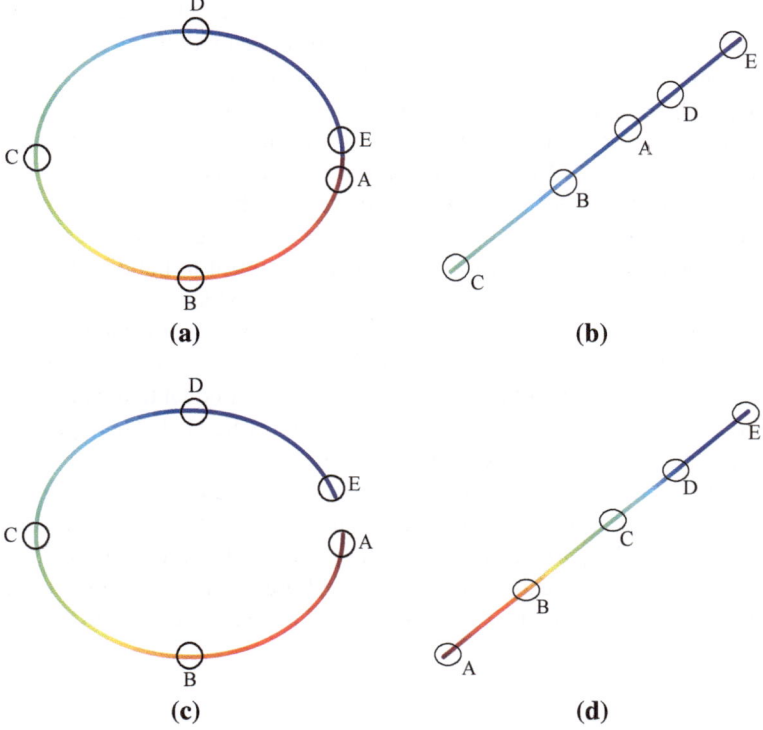

Fig. 3.3 A *circle* (**a**) is a 1-dimensional manifold embedded in 2-dimensional space that contains a non-contractable loop. When embedded into 1-dimensional space the manifold is embedded on *top* of itself (**b**). However, by introducing a small tear in the manifold (**c**), the 1-dimensional embedding is able to be recovered (**d**)

3.3.1 Manifolds with Loops

Some manifolds that exhibit topologies such as non-contractable loops cannot be embedded into the target dimensionality without introducing distortions. An example of this is the circle manifold shown in Fig. 3.3. The circle shown in Fig. 3.3 is a 1-manifold, however, at least 2 dimensions are needed to embed the circle and preserve its topological structure. Manifold with so called 'essential loops' can be effectively embedded by applying a manifold tearing [19] pre-processing step. Returning to the circle shown in Fig. 3.3, the basic idea of manifold tearing is to 'cut' the manifold at some point so that it can be embedded in 1-dimensional space. The fact that nonlinear spectral dimensionality reduction methods use a graph as a representation of the underlying manifold becomes useful when considering how to tear the manifold.

A non-contractible loop can be related to a non-contractible cycle in a graph [19] and so manifold tearing seeks to replace the standard graph used for spectral dimensionality reduction with one that contains no non-contractible cycles. This is achieved by condensing the neighbourhood graph down to a form that is guaranteed to contain no non-contractible cycles. This can be done by utilising a spanning tree, either a Minimum Spanning Tree (MST) [11, 20] or a Shortest Path Tree (SPT) [21]. Given a graph $G = \langle V, E \rangle$ with a vertex set corresponding to the original dataset and edges being introduced as a result of a k-nearest neighbour graph method, a spanning tree $G_T = \langle V, E_T \rangle$ is a subgraph of G with a reduced edge set, $E_T \subset E$, that is a tree (i.e. a connected graph with no cycles). The graph G_T may contain no non-contractible cycles but it is not densely connected enough to fully reconstruct the data [22]. Therefore, edges that were discarded as a result of building the spanning tree are reintroduced into a new graph $G_C = \langle V, E_C \rangle$, which is initialised with G_T. The edges are considered according to a breadth first traversal of G along its spanning tree G_T. The edges are only added to G_C if the number of edges of the shortest cycle generated by the addition of the new edge is less than or equal to a parameter value c, the maximum number of edges in an elementary cycle [19]. The algorithm then terminates when the breadth first search has completed.

One of the drawbacks of the manifold tearing procedure is that it does not work on 'spherical' manifolds since they do not contain non-contractible loops. However, the adjustment of the parameter c does allow for two different types of tear to be produced—min and max tears. This allows for different numbers of non-contractible cycles to be broken and so allows for the method to be adapted to different types of manifold.

3.3.2 Multiple Manifolds

An interesting yet often overlooked area within dimensionality reduction is the case where the data is drawn from multiple manifolds, that is, rather than the data being sampled from a single manifold, $\mathbf{X} \subset \mathcal{M}$, it is in fact made up of data sampled from more than one manifold, $\mathbf{X} = \{\mathbf{X}_1, \mathbf{X}_2, \ldots, \mathbf{X}_p\}$ where $\mathbf{X}_1 \subset \mathcal{M}, \mathbf{X}_2 \subset \mathcal{N}, \ldots, \mathbf{X}_p \subset \mathcal{Q}$. Without extensions, traditional spectral dimensionality reduction methods will often fail to recover the underlying manifolds of such datasets.

One of the simplest solutions to such a problem is to apply a clustering algorithm to the data *prior* to performing dimensionality reduction and then reduce the dimensionality of each cluster separately. In the trivial example given above, this would result in p separate embeddings for each of the subsets of $\mathbf{X}$. There are however two key problems with such an approach. Firstly, it works on the assumption that the clustering algorithm used is able to successfully recover the correct partitioning of the data into disjoint manifolds. This may not always be the case since clustering algorithms themselves will make assumptions about the underlying geometry of the data. If the partitioning of the data by the clustering algorithm is not correct, then the subsequent dimensionality reduction will contain errors since data corresponding to different manifolds will be assigned to other disjoint areas. It is worth noting however that there is a small body of work concerned with utilising manifold structure as part of the clustering problem (e.g. [23, 24]) which may go some way to alleviating the problems associated with multi-manifold learning, however, they do not address all the problems.

The second key problem with this simplistic approach is that the embeddings will all be given in different co-ordinate spaces with no mapping available between them. Returning once again to the trivial example given above, if each of the disjoint subsets of $\mathbf{X}$ have been embedded into a low-dimensional space such that there are p embeddings. $\mathbf{Y}_1, \mathbf{Y}_2, \ldots, \mathbf{Y}_p$, then any spatial relations between each of these embeddings is lost. There is no way of telling how points drawn from the manifold embedded in $\mathbf{Y}_2$ are related spatially to those embedded in say $\mathbf{Y}_3$. As such, it is apparent that more sophisticated techniques are needed to overcome these two problems and adequately deal with multiple manifolds.

One such algorithm that seeks to overcome the above problems was presented in [25] that uses Isomap [1] as the core spectral dimensionality reduction algorithm, however, it is possible that the method could be extended to other algorithms. The proposed method, known as M-Isomap, has two main steps. First, the data is clustered into p manifolds using a novel k-edge connected components method. Each of the p manifolds are then embedded into their respective low-dimensional embeddings, at the same time the skeleton structure of the dataset is built and preserved in the low-dimensional space. The second step is then to 'align' each of the p manifolds in the low-dimensional space by referring to the skeleton produced in step one. Although the results show that this method can be an efficient way of modelling multiple manifolds on both synthetic and real data, it is still heavily reliant on an initial neighbourhood size parameter. As some of the results in [25] show, if the neighbourhood size is over approximated then the manifolds will overlap. So for this method to be truly effective it should be used in conjunction with an appropriate neighbourhood size parameter estimation method.

Another similar algorithm is Sparse Manifold Clustering and Embedding (SMCE) [26] which simultaneously clusters and embeds the data. As opposed to the previously described method [25], SMCE allows for automatic selection of neighbours as well as simultaneous clustering and embedding in a unified manner. The heart of SMCE is an optimisation program that seeks to learn a small selection of neighbours for each data point that span a low-dimensional subspace passing near that point. The non-zero elements of the solution to this sparse representation indicate the points that lie on the same manifold, thus clustering the data points. On top of this, the weights associated with the chosen neighbours indicate the distances which can be subsequently used for dimensionality reduction based on Laplacian Eigenmaps [2].

One boundary case when considering multiple manifold algorithms is when the different manifolds contain different intrinsic dimensionality. This is a problem that is addressed in [27], however the solution given does not directly address spectral dimensionality reduction. It does however contain principles that could be translated into the domain of spectral dimensionality reduction. The method works by associating a probability density with each manifold and then representing the collection of manifolds by a mixture of their associated density models. Although the method

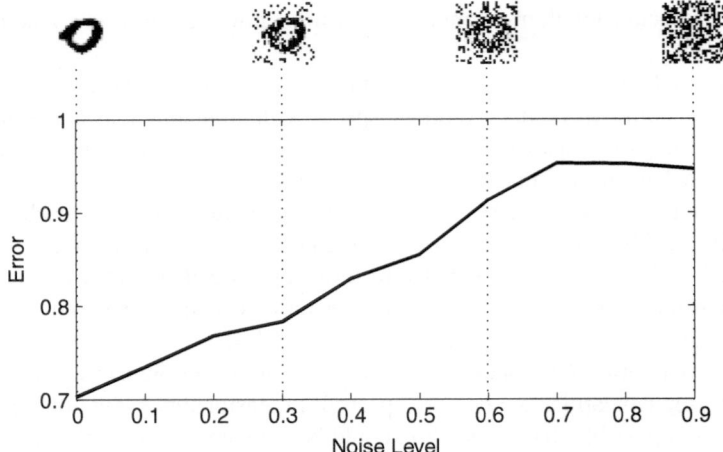

Fig. 3.4 The low-dimensional embedding of the MNIST digit '0' was found using Isomap ($k = 12, n = 980, d = 2$). As the noise level increases, the error, measured as $1 - \rho$ (where ρ is the residual variance), also increases indicating an inaccurate low-dimensional embedding

in [27] is based on Generative-Topographic Mapping (GTM) [28], it is possible that such a method could be used after learning multiple manifolds so as to bring them together within a single model.

3.4 Noise and Outliers

It is not unreasonable to expect data drawn from real world experiments to contain high levels of noise and/or outliers. Spectral dimensionality reduction methods are highly susceptible to noise, as shown in Fig. 3.4. As the noise level increases the measured performance of spectral dimensionality reduction decreases. This is not surprising as high noise levels will make it difficult for the underlying manifold to be adequately and accurately modelled. Therefore, there is need for methods to be used that enable spectral dimensionality reduction methods to be employed in the presence of noisy data.

Existing methods for dealing with noise can be broadly split into two categories: those that act as a pre-processing step prior to performing dimensionality reduction, and those that incorporate noise reduction as part of an existing or novel dimensionality reduction algorithm. There is obviously more effectiveness in terms of generalisation when considering the former methods, however, by explicitly adding noise reduction to existing or novel algorithms it is possible to build a more robust approach to handling noise.

3.4.1 Pre-processing Methods

Two existing methods that act as a pre-processing step are local smoothing [29] and manifold denoising [30]. Local smoothing is an iterative method that smooths the dataset at a local level using a weighted PCA approach. As well as this, the methodology also incorporates outlier handling through the exploitation of a Minimum Spanning Tree (MST). The method performs local smoothing by iteratively projecting all the points onto their local subspace, as found by weighted PCA, and then moving the outliers towards the nearest 'patch' on the manifold. The method begins by computing the k-nearest neighbours for each point $\mathbf{x}_i$ in $\mathbf{X}$ denoted by the set $\mathcal{N}_i$. To detect outliers, the MST is formed from the weighted graph, $G = \langle V, E, W \rangle$, which is calculated over the neighbourhood set $\mathcal{N}_i$ where V is the vertex set of the nearest neighbours of $\mathbf{x}_i$ including $\mathbf{x}_i$ itself, E is the edge set, and W is the weights corresponding to each edge in E calculated according to the Euclidean distance between the two connected vertices. The MST produces a reduced edge set $E' \subseteq E$ and associated weight set $W' \subseteq W$ with the minimum total edge weights. Once the MST has been formed, the average edge weight, $\bar{W}'$, is then calculated; if the maximum edge weight is much greater than $\bar{W}'$ then the MST is split into two subgraphs $G_1 = \langle V_1, E_1 \rangle$ and $G_2 = \langle V_2, E_2 \rangle$, this is done by disconnecting the largest edge. If the maximum edge weight in the subgraph containing $\mathbf{x}_i$ is much greater than $\bar{W}'$ then $\mathbf{x}_i$ is identified as an outlier. If identified as an outlier, the point is moved in the direction of one of the patches according to

$$\mathbf{x}_i^* = \alpha \mathbf{x}_i + (1 - \alpha)\mathbf{x}_t, \quad 0 < \alpha < 1 \tag{3.5}$$

$$t = \arg\max\{W(e'_{1a}), W(e'_{1b})\} \tag{3.6}$$

If $\mathbf{x}_i$ is not detected as an outlier then it is projected onto an affine subspace which is computed using a Weighted PCA algorithm. The outlier detection and affine subspace projection steps are repeated until the algorithm converges.

Similar to local smoothing is the manifold de-noising algorithm [30] which uses the graph Laplacian as the generator of a diffusion process that can be used to de-noise the manifold. Manifold de-noising is an iterative algorithm that re-computes the neighbourhood relations and the graph Laplacian at each step. Given a neighbourhood size value, k, and also a time step size δ, manifold de-noising seeks to update the solution at time step $(t + 1)$ according to

$$\mathbf{X}_{(t+1)} = (\mathbf{I} + \delta \mathbf{L})^{-1} \mathbf{X}_{(t)} \tag{3.7}$$

where $\mathbf{L}$ is the graph Laplacian built from a weighted neighbourhood graph with weights defined as

$$\mathbf{W}_{ij} = \exp\left(\frac{||\mathbf{X}_i - \mathbf{X}_j||^2}{(\max\{h(\mathbf{X}_i), h(\mathbf{X}_j)\})^2}\right) \tag{3.8}$$

if $||\mathbf{X}_i - \mathbf{X}_j||^2 \leq \max\{h(\mathbf{X}_i), h(\mathbf{X}_j)\}$. Here, $h(\mathbf{X}_i)$ denotes the k-nearest neighbour distances of $\mathbf{X}_i$. The problem of deciding a stopping criteria for manifold de-noising is an open ended one. The simplest method would be to stop when the changes in the samples fall below a certain threshold. More involved stopping criteria include stopping if the number of connected components in the graph increases, this is based on the intuition that if the diffusion process is allowed to continue indefinitely then the data becomes fully disconnected and forms into local clusters. Another proposed stopping criteria is to exploit the intrinsic dimensionality of the data which must be provided a priori. The manifold de-noising algorithm can stop if the correlation dimension [31] is equal to the supplied intrinsic dimensionality.

One of the major drawbacks of the manifold de-noising algorithm is that the k-nearest neighbour graph and the graph Laplacian need to be re-computed at each time step. As such, for large datasets the manifold de-noising algorithm may be inappropriate due to its increased computational cost.

3.4.2 Noise Handling Extensions

Due to its popularity, it is desirable to find a way for improved noise handling for Principal Components Analysis (PCA) [32]. One of the most widely cited and, in terms of other spectral dimensionality reduction, most useful methods is robust PCA [33]. Robust PCA is based on weighted PCA, where weights are assigned to each of the data points, but gives a measure of how likely it is that each data point was drawn from the underlying subspace. These likelihood measures can then be used to identify any outliers in the data [34].

Standard PCA seeks to find the least squares estimate of a displacement vector, $\mathbf{d}$, and orthonormal basis matrix, $\mathbf{Q}$, by minimising

$$\varepsilon = \sum_{i=1}^{n} ||\mathbf{x}_i - (\mathbf{d} + \mathbf{Q}\mathbf{Q}^T(\mathbf{x}_i - \mathbf{d}))||^2 \tag{3.9}$$

This optimisation can be further improved by using a weighted form, that is, for each data point, $\mathbf{x}_i$, a non-negative weight, α_i, is assigned. The weighted squared error criteria is then given as

$$\varepsilon_{\mathrm{w}} = \sum_{i=1}^{n} \alpha_i ||\mathbf{x}_i - (\mathbf{d} + \mathbf{Q}\mathbf{Q}^T(\mathbf{x}_i - \mathbf{d}))||^2 \tag{3.10}$$

with respect to $\mathbf{d}$ and $\mathbf{Q}$. It can be shown that the least squares estimate of $\mathbf{d}$ is given as the weighted sample mean vector [34], and the least squares estimate of the orthonormal basis vectors in $\mathbf{Q}$ are given by the top eigenvectors of the weighted sample covariance matrix.

What is readily apparent is that under the weighted PCA scheme the relative influence of data points that are considered as outliers should be low (i.e. small weight values). However, this assumes that the set of all weights $\Omega = \{\alpha_i\}_{i=1}^n$ are already known, this is not the case as the data should dictate the weights required for each point. As such, an iterative method—iteratively weighted least squares [35]—is employed to compute the least squares estimates as well as learn the corresponding weights.

Robust PCA is a good way of reducing the influence of outliers, which is traditionally a shortcoming of PCA. More than that, it provides the basis for a modified form of LLE [7]—Robust LLE [34]. Robust LLE utilises a local version of robust PCA to assign weight values to each point in a neighbourhood. These weight values are used to identify how likely it is that a given data point is an outlier and can be used to reduce the influence of the outliers on the final embedding result [34]. For each neighbourhood of k data points, robust PCA is performed to obtain a set of weights, $\{\alpha_i\}_{i=1}^k$. That is, for a given point $\mathbf{x}_i$, each of its k-nearest neighbours, $\{\mathbf{x}_{i_j}\}_{j=1}^k \in \mathbf{X}_{\mathcal{N}_i}$ has an associated weight (i.e. α_{i_j} is the weight associated with the neighbour $\mathbf{x}_{i_j}$). A reliability measure for each of the k-neighbours is then formed by computing the normalised weight values, $\alpha_j^* = \alpha_j / \sum_{p=1}^k \alpha_p$. For all points not in the neighbourhood of $\mathbf{x}_i$, their weights are set to 0. Running robust PCA on all data points in $\mathbf{X}$ gives rise to a complete set of normalised weights for all neighbourhoods. From this complete set of normalised weights a total reliability score s_i is obtained for each point $\mathbf{x}_i$ by summing all the normalised weight values. Intuitively, the smaller the value of the total reliability the more likely it is that $\mathbf{x}_i$ is an outlier. As such, a threshold, β, can be introduced such that only those points with reliability scores $s_i > \beta$ are used to obtain the low-dimensional embedding. This new set of "clean" points is denoted $\mathbf{X}'$.

Once the clean points have been identified, LLE is performed with a modified embedding cost function:

$$\Phi(\mathbf{Y}) = \sum_i s_i \left\| \mathbf{y}_i - \sum_j \mathbf{W}'_{ij} \mathbf{y}_j \right\|^2 \tag{3.11}$$

where $\mathbf{W}'$ denotes the weight matrix formed from $\mathbf{X}'$ according to Eq. 2.9. Notice that this is a modified form of Eq. 2.10 with the reliability scores adding an extra weighting. The R-LLE algorithm shows real improvement of standard LLE [34] but with added computational cost. The cost of finding the weights using robust PCA is high since an iterative approach is used to find weights for each point. It is also reliant on a parameter β which determines whether or not a point should be considered an outlier or not. It is easy to appreciate that an incorrect value of β could lead to errors in the embedding by over or under compensating for noise.

Another variant of LLE that aims to better handle noise is Neighbourhood Smoothing Embedding (NSE) [36]. NSE is a noise reducing variant of LLE that utilises local linear surface estimators [37] to obtain a more accurate representation of the local manifold with respect to noise. The NSE algorithm follows the same steps as LLE (see Sect. 2.3.4) but computes the weight matrix from the neighbourhoods *after* performing local linear surface estimation. The local linear surface estimation algorithm is a jump preserving surface fitting procedure, that is, if there is a sharp change in the surface (i.e. jump), that jump will be maintained during fitting. There is one drawback of the NSE approach in that it adds two new parameters that need to be considered. These parameters adjust the bandwidth of the kernel used for local linear surface estimation and also a threshold parameter. The results are promising for NSE [36], however, there is little discussion into the relative influence of these new parameters, so it is difficult to ascertain a full picture of the usefulness of the algorithm.

3.5 Summary

There is no doubt as to the importance of the various open problems discussed in this chapter. If the initial 'manifold modelling' stage is inadequate then the final embedding produced as a result of performing spectral dimensionality reduction will itself be inadequate. Therefore, it is important to spend time attempting to understand the nature of the data used and making decisions based on whether the data is expected to be highly noisy, contain loops, or lie on multiple manifolds. Thankfully, there are solutions to help overcome these data problems albeit at an extra computational cost.

One of the issues with the solutions described in this chapter is that in a real world setting they cannot be considered in isolation. For example, given a noisy dataset, a neighbourhood graph may need to be induced to de-noise the data. However, this neighbourhood graph requires a neighbourhood size parameter such as k, for which various estimators exist, but all of which will be affected by the presence of noise. As such, to obtain an estimate of k for the de-noising algorithm, the data first needs to be de-noised to get an accurate estimate. And so a cyclical dependency begins to build between the different approaches described in this chapter. This may not be a problem for datasets that are relatively small as the various approaches can be run multiple times with different parameters if need be. For larger datasets this may not be feasible, and so the cyclical dependency becomes more prominent and more difficult to deal with.

References

1. Tenenbaum, J.B., de Silva, V., Langford, J.C.: A global geometric framework for nonlinear dimensionality reduction. Science **290**, 2319–2322 (2000)
2. Belkin, M., Niyogi, P.: Laplacian eigenmaps and spectral techniques for embedding and clustering. In: Advances in Neural Information Processing Systems 14: Proceedings of the 2002 Conference (NIPS), pp. 585–591 (2002)
3. Garcia, V., Debreuve, E., Barlaud, M.: Fast k nearest neighbor search using GPU. Computer Vision and Pattern Recognition, Workshop pp. 1–6 (2008)

4. Kleinberg, J.M.: Two algorithms for nearest-neighbor search in high dimensions. In: Proceedings of the twenty-ninth annual ACM symposium on Theory of computing, STOC '97, pp. 599–608 (1997)
5. Nene, S.A., Nayar, S.K.: A simple algorithm for nearest neighbour search in high dimensions. IEEE Transactions on Pattern Analysis and Machine Intelligence 19(9), 989–1003 (1997)
6. Samko, O., Marshall, A.D., Rosin, P.: Selection of the optimal parameter value for the Isomap algorithm. Pattern Recognition Letters 27(9), 968–979 (2006)
7. Roweis, S.T., Saul, L.K.: Nonlinear dimensionality reduction by Locally Linear Embedding. Science 290, 2323–2326 (2000)
8. Kouropteva, O., Okun, O., Pietikainen, M.: Selection of the optimal parameter value for the locally linear embedding algorithm. In: Proceedings of the First International Conference on Fuzzy Systems and Knowledge Discovery, pp. 359–363 (2002)
9. Yang, L.: Building k edge-disjoint spanning trees of minimum total length for isometric data embedding. IEEE Transactions on Pattern Analysis and Machine Intelligence 27(10), 1680–1683 (2005)
10. Wen, G., Jiang, L., Shadbolt, N.R.: Using graph algebra to optimize neighborhood for isometric mapping. In: 20th International Joint Conference on Artificial Intelligence, pp. 2398–2403 (2007)
11. Kruskal, J.: On the shortest spanning subtree of a graph and the travelling salesman problem. Proceedings of the American Mathematical Society 7(1), 48–50 (1956)
12. Fischer, B., Buhmann, J.M.: Bagging for path-based clustering. IEEE Transactions on Pattern Analysis and Machine Intelligence 25(1), 1411–1415 (2003)
13. Fischer, B., Buhmann, J.M.: Path-based clustering for grouping of smooth curves and texture segmentation. IEEE Transactions on Pattern Analysis and Machine Intelligence 25(4), 513–518 (2003)
14. Zhang, Z., Zha, H.: Principal manifolds and nonlinear dimension reduction via local tangent space alignment. SIAM Journal on Scientific Computing 26(1), 313–338 (2004)
15. Wang, J., Zhang, Z., Zha, H.: Adaptive manifold learning. In: Advances in Neural Information Processing Systems 16: Proceedings of the 2004 Conference (NIPS), pp. 1473–1480 (2004)
16. Zhang, Z., Wang, J., Zha, H.: Adaptive Manifold Learning. IEEE Transactions on Pattern Analysis and Machine Intelligence 34(2), 253–265 (2012)
17. Mekuz, N., Tsotsos, J.K.: Parameterless Isomap with adaptive neighborhood selection. In: Deutsche Arbeitsgemeinschaft für Mustererkennung DAGM, pp. 364–373 (2006)
18. Gao, Z., Liang, J.: The dynamical neighborhood selection based on the sampling density and manifold curvature for isometric data embedding. Pattern Recognition Letters 32, 202–209 (2011)
19. Lee, J.A., Verleysen, M.: Nonlinear dimensionality reduction of data manifolds with essential loops. Neurocomputing 67, 29–53 (2005)
20. Prim, R.C.: Shortes connection networks and some generalisations. Bell System Technical Journal 36, 1389–1401 (1957)
21. Dijkstra, E.W.: A note on two problems in connexion with graphs. Numerische Mathematik 1, 269–271 (1959)
22. Roychowdhury, S., Ghosh, J.: Robust Laplacian Eigenmaps using global information. In: Manifold Learning and Applications: Papers from the AAAI Fall Symposium (FS-09-04), pp. 42–49 (2009)
23. Gong, D., Zhao, X., Medioni, G.: Robust multiple manifolds structure learning. In: Proceedings of the 29th International Conference on Machine Learning (2012)
24. Guo, Q., Li, H., Chen, W., Shen, I.F., Parkkinen, J.: Manifold clustering via energy minimisation. In: Proceedings of the Sixth International Conference on Machine Learning and Applications (2007)
25. Fan, M., Qiao, H., Zhang, B., Zhang, X.: Isometric mult-manifold learning for feature extraction. In: Proceedings of the 12th International Conference on Data Mining, pp. 241–250 (2012)

26. Elhamifar, E., Vidal, R.: Sparse manifold clustering and embedding. In: Advances in Neural Information Processing Systems 24: Proceedings of the 2011 Conference (NIPS), pp. 55–63 (2011)
27. Wang, C., Mahadevan, S.: Manifold alignment using Procrustes analysis. In: Proceedings of the 25th International Conference on Machine Learning, Helsinki, Finland, pp. 1120–1127 (2008)
28. Bishop, C.M., Svensen, M., Williams, C.K.I.: Gtm: The generative topographic mapping. Neural Computation **10**, 215–234 (1998)
29. Park, J., Zhang, Z., Zha, H.: Local smoothing for manifold learning. In: Proceedings of the IEEE Computer Society Conference on Computer Vision and Pattern Recognition (CVPR), pp. II–452–II–459 Vol. 2 (2004)
30. Hein, M., Maier, M.: Manifold denoising. In: Advances in Neural Information Processing Systems 18: Proceedings of the 2006 Conference (NIPS) (2006)
31. Grassberger, P., Procaccia, I.: Measuring the strangeness of strange attractors. Physica **D9**(189), 189–208 (1983)
32. Joliffe, I.T.: Principal Component Analysis. Springer-Verlag, New York (1986)
33. de la Torre, F., Black, M.J.: A framework for robust subspace learning. International Journal of Computer Vision **54**(1/2/3), 117–142 (2003)
34. Chang, H., Yeung, D.Y.: Robust locally linear embedding. Pattern Recognition **39**, 1053–1065 (2006)
35. Holland, P.W., Welsch, R.E.: Robust regression using iteratively reweighted least squares. Communications in Statistics - Theory and Methods **6**(9), 813–827 (1977)
36. Yin, J., Hu, D., Zhou, Z.: Noisy manifold learning using neighborhood smoothing embedding. Pattern Recognition Letters **29**, 1613–1620 (2008)
37. Qiu, P.: The local piecewisely linear kernel smoothing procedure for fitting regression surfaces. Technometrics **46**, 87–98 (2004)

Chapter 4
Intrinsic Dimensionality

Abstract In this chapter, various approaches are considered to estimate the intrinsic dimensionality of datasets. These approaches look at the spectrum of eigenvalues and also local and global aspects of the data. In addition, limitations of existing dimensionality reduction approaches are discussed, especially with respect to the range of possible embedding dimensions and reduced performance at higher embedding dimensionalities.

Keywords Intrinsic dimensionality · Fractal dimension · Eigenspectrum

In this chapter the problems associated with intrinsic dimensionality are presented and discussed. In simple terms the intrinsic dimensionality of a dataset is the dimensionality of the manifold from which the dataset is drawn. There is obviously benefit in exploiting the intrinsic dimensionality of a dataset, however, there are significant problems associated with this area of spectral dimensionality reduction; namely, how is the intrinsic dimensionality estimated, and, perhaps more importantly, are there limits to the dimensionality that spectral dimensionality reduction algorithms can embed into? This chapter deals with each of these problems in turn and highlights some of the central algorithms used to estimate the intrinsic dimensionality of the data.

4.1 Background

Intrinsic dimensionality estimation is concerned with obtaining an estimate of the dimensionality of the manifold that is embedded in high-dimensional space. More often than not, although the dataset's ambient dimensionality may be high, its intrinsic dimensionality will be much lower. An example of this is shown in Fig. 4.1 where a sequence of 32×32 pixel images ($\mathbf{X} \in \mathbb{R}^{1024}$) are taken. The estimated intrinsic

H. Strange and R. Zwiggelaar, *Open Problems in Spectral Dimensionality Reduction*,
SpringerBriefs in Computer Science, DOI: 10.1007/978-3-319-03943-5_4,
© The Author(s) 2014

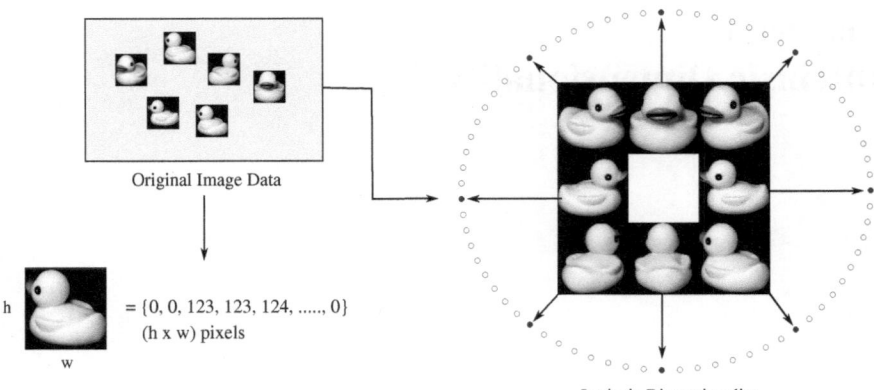

Original Image Data

h [duck image] $= \{0, 0, 123, 123, 124, \ldots, 0\}$
                    $(h \times w)$ pixels
w

Intrinsic Dimensionality

Fig. 4.1 An example of intrinsic dimensionality in the domain of imaging. A sequence of 72 images are taken of a rotating object [1], each image is 32×32 pixels in size thus creating a high-dimensional matrix of size 72×1024. Although the dimensionality of this matrix is high, since the only variation between each image is rotation, the intrinsic dimensionality of this dataset is 2, since it is only the angular rotation that is needed to describe the difference between each image

dimensionality of this dataset is much lower than the ambient dimensionality ($D = 1024$) since the variation between the images is simply the rotation angle of the object. Therefore, the intrinsic dimensionality of this dataset is 2, as shown by the low-dimensional embedding in Fig. 4.1.

Estimating the intrinsic dimensionality of a dataset is an important pre-processing step for spectral dimensionality reduction as embedding the dataset into its non-intrinsic dimensionality can lead to suboptimal performance of any subsequent algorithms [2]. As such, the area of intrinsic dimensionality estimation has attracted much attention over the years, especially since the advent of nonlinear spectral dimensionality reduction techniques.

4.2 Estimating Dimensionality: The Spectral Gap

For some spectral dimensionality reduction algorithms the intrinsic dimensionality can be estimated by examining the eigenspectrum of the feature matrix $\mathbf{F}$ (e.g. PCA, Isomap, MVU). In all such cases, the most prominent gap in the ordered list of eigenvalues is used to estimate the intrinsic dimensionality of the data. Throughout the following discussion Principal Components Analysis (PCA) [3] will be used as the exemplar spectral dimensionality reduction technique that exhibits the spectral gap property. Returning to the description of PCA from Sect. 2.2.1, PCA computes the eigenvectors $\mathbf{Q} = \{\mathbf{u}_1, \mathbf{u}_2, \ldots, \mathbf{u}_D\}$ and eigenvalues $\Lambda = \{\lambda_1, \lambda_2, \ldots, \lambda_D\}$ of the feature (covariance) matrix $\mathbf{F}$ (Eq. 2.2). Each of the eigenvectors corresponds to a principal axis of the data and the associated eigenvalues measure the variance of

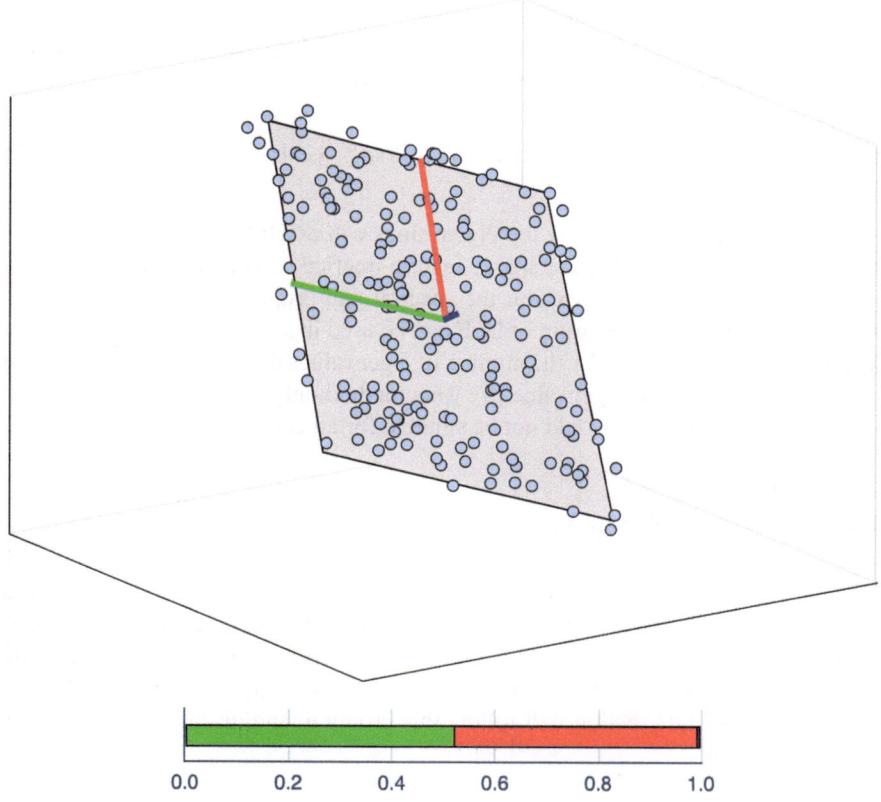

Fig. 4.2 A set of points noisily sampled from a plane in 3-dimensional space. Since the points are sampled from a plane, the intrinsic dimensionality of the data is expected to be $d = 2$. This is confirmed by the eigenspectrum of the data, where the difference in size between the first and second eigenvectors is small, whereas the difference in size between the second and third eigenvector is large. This 'spectral gap' gives rise to the estimated intrinsic dimensionality being $d = 2$

the data as projected along that principal axis. What becomes readily apparent is that the spectrum of the eigenvalues can reveal the intrinsic dimensionality of the low-dimensional *subspace* upon which the data lies. To better understand this consider the simple example shown in Fig. 4.2. A set of data points are noisily sampled from a 2-dimensional plane in 3-dimensional space and PCA is performed to obtain the eigenvalues and eigenvectors. Since the data lies on or near a 2-dimensional subspace there are only two significant eigenvalues; the variance of the data along the principal axis corresponding to the normal to the place being trivial. The number of significant eigenvalues therefore measures the dimensionality of the subspace that contains most of the variance of the data. The spectral gap then arises from the largest gap in the eigenvalue spectrum. In the example given in Fig. 4.2, the largest gap occurs between the second and third eigenvalue and so the intrinsic dimensionality of the subspace can be estimated as the lower bound of this gap (i.e. 2-dimensions).

Expanding this definition to D-dimensions is trivial. The gaps in the eigenspectrum are given by $|\lambda_{i-1} - \lambda_i|_{i=2}^{D}$ and so the largest of these gaps corresponds to the intrinsic dimensionality of the subspace and is given by

$$d = \underset{i=2}{\overset{D}{\mathrm{argmax}}} \, |\lambda_{i-1} - \lambda_i|_{i=2}^{D} - 1 \qquad (4.1)$$

All techniques that utilise the top eigenvalues will exhibit this spectral gap property, similarly, methods that use sparse feature matrices and therefore consider the bottom eigenvalues will not exhibit the spectral gap property [4]. Some work has suggested that the eigenspectrum of LLE can be used in a similar way by estimating the intrinsic dimensionality by the number of eigenvalues that compare in magnitude to the smallest non-zero eigenvalue [5]. This method only works in the most trivial of examples however and would not be suitable for all cases [6].

4.3 Estimating Dimensionality: Other Methods

When using those spectral dimensionality reduction methods that do not exhibit a prominent gap in the spectrum of eigenvalues other intrinsic dimensionality estimation methods need to be employed. A coarse split in these algorithms can be made by examining whether they estimate the intrinsic dimensionality at a local or a global scale. The rest of this section will follow this grouping and discuss the advantages of each approach.

4.3.1 Global Estimators

Global estimators of intrinsic dimensionality have a long history that extend out of the field of spectral dimensionality reduction. Possibly the most popular tool for estimating the intrinsic dimensionality of a dataset at a global scale is the fractal dimension [7], which can be thought of as a quantity that indicates how completely an object fills space as one moves to increasingly smaller scales [8]. Two methods that use this fractal dimension approach are Box-Counting [9, 10] and Correlation Dimension [11]. The Box-Counting method supposes that the input data $\mathbf{X}$ is normalised such that all the points reside inside the unit hyper-cube. If the hyper-cube is divided into r even intervals then D^r smaller hyper-cubes are created. Not all of these smaller hyper-cubes will contain datapoints as it is not expected that $\mathbf{X}$ fills the entire space. As such, $N(r)$ denotes the number of smaller hyper-cubes that contain *at least* one data point. Following from [8], the Box-Counting fractal dimension of $\mathbf{X}$ can then be define as

$$D_B \equiv \lim_{r \to \infty} \frac{\log N(r)}{\log r} \qquad (4.2)$$

From this measure, the intrinsic dimensionality can be expressed as

$$d = \frac{\log N(r)}{\log r} - \frac{\log c}{\log r} \tag{4.3}$$

where c is a constant that expresses the proportionality of $N(r)$ and r^d such that $N(r) = c \cdot r^d$. In practice the intrinsic dimensionality is estimated from a plot of $\log N(r)$ versus $\log r$ and then estimating the slope of the linear part of the curve [8]. One of the immediate problems with the Box-Counting method is that it is computationally inefficient for datasets with large dimensionality. This is because the algorithmic complexity grows exponentially with the original dimensionality D [12]. As such, the correlation dimension [11] is a useful and computationally simpler substitue for the Box-Counting dimension.

The correlation dimension method builds on the idea of the correlation integral, defined as

$$C_m(r) = \frac{2}{n(n-1)} \sum_{i=1}^{n} \sum_{j=i+1}^{n} I(\|\mathbf{x}_j - \mathbf{x}_i\| \leq r) \tag{4.4}$$

where I is an indicator function such that $I(\lambda)$ is 1 iff the condition λ holds, otherwise 0. The correlation integral can be thought of as the mean probability that the distance of a pair of points is less than or equal to r. The correlation dimension is therefore defined as

$$D_C \equiv \lim_{n \to \infty} \lim_{r \to \infty} \frac{\log C_m(r)}{\log r} \tag{4.5}$$

As with the Box-Counting dimension, the intrinsic dimension can be estimated from the correlation dimension by examining the plot of $\log C_m(r)$ versus $\log r$ and estimating the linear part of the curve.

One of the questions raised when using fractal methods such as those described above is how many data points are needed to gain an accurate estimate of the intrinsic dimensionality? This question was addressed in [13] and [14] where it was shown that, for a dataset in D-dimensional space, then at least $10^{D/2}$ data points are needed to accurately estimate the intrinsic dimensionality. It is quickly apparent that even for comparatively low-dimensional datasets, large values of n are needed (i.e. for $D = 10$, n is suggested to be 10^5). There are however methods for improving the reliability of fractal dimension methods for low values of n. For example, using a bootstrap [15] approach called surrogate data [16], a synthetic dataset is created that matches the statistical properties of $\mathbf{X}$ but has a far larger number of data points. However, this method does become computationally expensive for large values of D and will also be unable to re-produce the manifold properties of the data using only simple statistical measures.

The above global intrinsic dimensionality estimation techniques all rely on the fractal dimension to gain an estimated intrinsic dimensionality value. This is not the only way of using global information to gain an intrinsic dimensionality estimate as shown in the Geodesic Minimum Spanning Tree method (GMST) [17]. Given a geodesic distance graph, as computed in a similar way to the Isomap algorithm (See Sect. 2.3.1), the intrinsic dimensionality is estimated by computing multiple Minimum Spanning Trees (MSTs) from the geodesic graph and then computing the length functional using a linear least squares method. The key insight of the GMST method is that the growth rate of the length functional of this graph is strongly dependent on the intrinsic dimension d and as such can lead to an estimate of the intrinsic dimensionality of the data [17].

The basic GMST algorithm for intrinsic dimensionality estimation can briefly be described as follows. Given a set of q integers, $A = \{a_1, a_2, \ldots, a_q\}$ where $1 \leq a_1 \leq a_2 \leq \ldots \leq a_q \leq n$, let N be an integer such that $N/n = \rho$ for some $\rho \in (0, 1]$. For each value of $a \in A$, a random dataset, $\mathbf{X}_a$, is drawn with replacement where the a data points within each set are drawn from $\mathbf{X}$ independently. From these samples the empirical mean of the GMST length functionals are computed according to

$$\mathbf{L}_a = N^{-1} \sum_{j=1}^{N} \hat{\mathbf{L}}(\mathbf{X}_a^j) \tag{4.6}$$

where $\hat{\mathbf{L}}$ is the geodesic minimal graph length. This can then be formed into a linear model given $\mathbf{l} = [\log(\mathbf{L}_{a1}), \ldots, \log(\mathbf{L}_{aq})]$ where

$$\mathbf{A} = \begin{bmatrix} \log(a_1) & \ldots & \log(a_q) \\ 1 & \ldots & 1 \end{bmatrix}^T \tag{4.7}$$

and

$$\mathbf{l} = \mathbf{A} \begin{bmatrix} b \\ c \end{bmatrix} + \varepsilon \tag{4.8}$$

where $b = (d - \gamma)/d$ and $c = \log \beta_d + \gamma/d H_\alpha(f)$. Here c relates to the entropy of the data which for the purpose of intrinsic dimensionality estimation is not required. To gain an estimate of d a methods-of-moments approach is used such that the estimate of d can be obtained according to

$$d = \text{round}\{\gamma/(1 - \hat{b})\} \tag{4.9}$$

given that $\hat{b}$ is an estimate of b. Repeating the above approach a number of times independently over $\mathbf{X}$ will given a range of estimates for d which can be averaged to give an overall estimate of the intrinsic dimensionality of the data. The GMST method is able to make estimates of d without requiring reconstructing the entire manifold and it does produce a global estimate of the intrinsic dimensionality. However, it does make the assumption that the embedding is isometric and so would not be suitable for non-isometric Riemannian manifolds [17].

4.3.2 Local Estimators

The methods described in Sect. 4.3.1 assume that the intrinsic dimensionality of the data can be accurately estimated at a global scale, that is, using global properties. However, there are numerous algorithms for estimating the intrinsic dimensionality by examining local properties of the data.

Possibly the simplest of all of these local estimation methods is based on the ideas presented in [18] where a variant of Eq. 4.1 is employed over local regions of the data. However, the actual method presented in [18] requires many decisions from the user to obtain an estimate of the intrinsic dimensionality. The basic premise can however be extended to an unsupervised approach by employing Eq. 4.1 over local neighbourhoods of $\mathbf{X}$. Consider a partitioning, S, of $\mathbf{X}$ into m subsets such that $S = \{\mathbf{X}_1, \mathbf{X}_2, \ldots, \mathbf{X}_m\}$. Here, the partitioning can be found using clustering or another suitable approach (i.e. the k-nearest neighbours of each $\mathbf{x}_i$). The intrinsic dimensionality of each of the subsets in S is then calculated using Eq. 4.1 leading to a range of estimates. From this range of estimates the intrinsic dimension can be estimated using a measure such as the mean or median of the range.

The nearest-neighbour algorithm [19, 20] examines the distances between points at a local scale to estimate the intrinsic dimensionality. The original definition of the nearest-neighbour estimator was given in [19] as

$$d = \frac{\bar{r}_k}{(\bar{r}_{k+1} - \bar{r}_k)k} \tag{4.10}$$

where $\bar{r}_k$ is the average distance from each data point to its kth neighbour. However, as noted in [20], this is a biased estimator even in the simplest of cases and therefore a modified algorithm based on Eq. 4.10 was presented. The method evaluates $\bar{r}_k$ over a range of k from $k_{\min}$ to $k_{\max}$ and a least square regression line is fitted to $\bar{r}_k$ as a function of $(\bar{r}_{k+1} - \bar{r}_k)$ [20]. The modified nearest-neighbour estimator can then be obtained as

$$d = \left(\sum_{k=k_{\min}}^{k_{\max}-1} (\bar{r}_k + 1 - \bar{r}_j)^2 \right)^{-1} \left(\sum_{k=k_{\min}}^{k_{\max}-1} \frac{(\bar{r}_{k+1} - \bar{r} - k)\bar{r}_k}{k} \right) \tag{4.11}$$

The main drawback of both of the nearest-neighbour algorithms for intrinsic dimensionality estimation is that they assume the neighbours are locally uniformly distributed. As well as this, they have a drastic tendency to underestimate the intrinsic dimensionality especially when the intrinsic dimensionality is 'high' [20].

Another local approach to intrinsic dimensionality estimation is to apply maximum likelihood to the distance between near neighbours [21]. The central idea of the maximum likelihood estimator (MLE) is to fix a point $\mathbf{x}_i$, and then treat the near-neighbours around that point as a homogeneous Poisson process in that neighbourhood. As shown in [21], the MLE can be reduced to

$$
\hat{d}_k = \left[\frac{1}{k-1} \sum_{j=1}^{k-1} \log \frac{T_k(\mathbf{x}_i)}{T_j(\mathbf{x}_i}} \right]^{-1}
\tag{4.12}
$$

where $T_k(\mathbf{x}_i)$ is equal to the Euclidean distance between $\mathbf{x}_i$ and its k-th nearest neighbour. MLE has proved to be a popular technique for intrinsic dimensionality estimation thanks in part to its relatively fast computation speed. As mention in [21], it does however suffer from negative bias in high-dimensions, a problem suffered by many intrinsic dimensionality reduction techniques.

For all of the above local estimators a parameter needs to be supplied to define at what local scale the dimensionality should be estimated. This means that there can be a link between local intrinsic dimensionality reduction estimators and the neighbourhood-size problem encountered in the previous chapter. However, one approach that can be employed to overcome this problem is to use a multi-scale approach, where the intrinsic dimensionality is estimated over a range of neighbourhood sizes. This is similar to the approach originally suggested in [20] and shown in Eq. 4.11. Although it adds processing time, it does overcome the problem of seeking to find a single neighbourhood size value. By examining the intrinsic dimensionality estimate over a range of neighbourhood size values a potentially more robust estimate can be obtained without being tied down to a single neighbourhood size value.

A local intrinsic dimensionality estimator that does not explicitly require a neighbourhood size value is the incising balls method [22]. The basic premise of the algorithm is to use a set of balls that incise the manifold, with each of these 'incising balls' containing a set number of data points and a radius. The intrinsic dimensionality of the dataset can then be estimated by evaluating the polynomial relationship of the radius of a ball and the number of data points within the ball [22].

The basic incising balls algorithm contains three main steps:

1. Firstly, the Euclidean distance matrix $\mathbf{D}$ is computed over all data points such that $D_{ij} = ||\mathbf{x}_i - \mathbf{x}_j||^2$. This distance matrix is analysed to compute the maximum radius R of the incising balls. The value of R is inferred by obtaining the frequency histogram of all the distances and then setting R to be equal to the highest apex of this histogram. The minimum radius, r, is set to be $r = \min(\mathbf{D})$.
2. A set of m incising balls are then formed with radius

$$
\phi_i = r + \frac{i(R-r)}{m} \quad \text{for } i = 1, 2, \ldots m
\tag{4.13}
$$

and volume

$$v_i = \frac{1}{n} \sum_{k=1}^{n} \sum_{l=1}^{n} I(\mathbf{d}_{kl} < \phi_i) \quad \text{for } i = 1, 2, \ldots m \qquad (4.14)$$

where I is the indicator function.

3. The final step is to use a least squares fitting method to find fitting poly-
   nomials based on the values $\{(\phi_i, v_i)\}_{i=1}^{n}$. The best data fitting polynomial,
   $v = \sum_{i=1}^{t} \beta_i \phi_i$, is found by assessing them one by one from degree $\min\{m, D\}$
   to degree one until the first one satisfying the following conditions is found:

   a. $\beta_t > 0$ and β_t is greater than a significance value α usually set as 0.01 [22].
   b. Given

   $$\beta_{\max} = \max_{1 \le j \le t} \beta_j \qquad (4.15)$$

   then $|\beta_{\max}/\beta_t| < C$ for a given constant C where $C < 10^4$.

Given that the i-th fitting polynomial satisfies the above criteria, the final intrinsic
dimensionality can be estimated as $d = q + i$ where q is the degree of the best
data fitting polynomial.

The incising balls method is more robust at dealing with high-dimensional data
than the MLE [21] however the computational cost is higher. The overall complexity
of the incising balls method is $O(n^2)$ which can be reduced to $O(nL)$ if an approximation method is used whereby the distances between n and L landmark points is
used in Step 1.

4.4 Choosing Techniques and Limitations

As with dimensionality reduction techniques themselves, there is no gold standard
intrinsic dimensionality estimator. Instead, questions need to be asked prior to using
an intrinsic dimensionality estimator so as to help the user gain a meaningful and
useful result.

To show the relative performance of some intrinsic dimensionality estimation
techniques, each technique is used to estimate the dimensionality of a set of points
sampled from the surface of a p-dimensional unit sphere. Figure 4.3 shows the
result of estimating the dimensionality of a p-dimensional sphere from $p = 2$ to
$p = 60$. What is immediately apparent is that as the dimensionality of the p-sphere
increases, a negative bias is observed among all estimators. That is, the estimated
intrinsic dimensionality is far below the actual dimensionality. This negative bias
is observed among all intrinsic dimensionality estimators but is most pronounced
among local estimators. The reason for this can be attributed to the assumption
made by local estimators that sufficiently large numbers of samples fall within the
local region being considered. This assumption requires a large number of samples
in high-dimensions for an accurate intrinsic dimensionality estimate to be obtained

Fig. 4.3 Intrinsic
dimensionality estimates
from three different methods. As the dimensionality of
the *p*-sphere increases, the
negative bias of all intrinsic
dimensionality estimation
techniques becomes more
pronounced

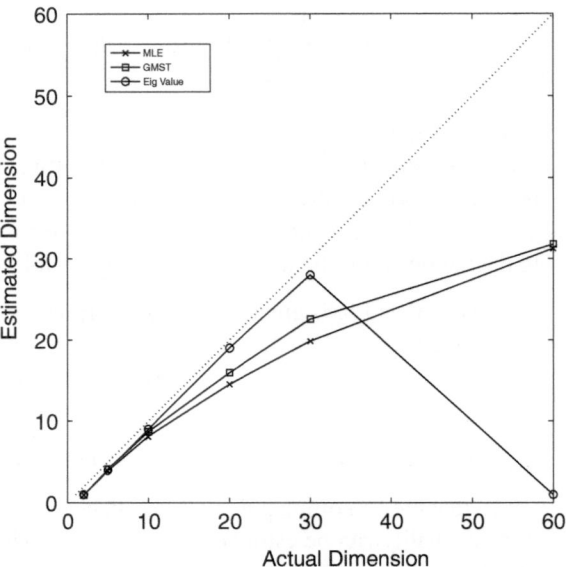

[21], but this is not always possible nor is it desirable as it increases the computational
complexity.

It is worthwhile ending this chapter with a word of caution; what is often left unad-
dressed in the manifold learning literature is the question of whether dimensionality
reduction algorithms are capable of embedding data into dimensions greater than four
or five. This question was posed in [23] and has been left tantalisingly unanswered.
The problem arises due to the fact that, when the embedding space exceeds four
or five (i.e. the intrinsic dimensionality of the data exceeds these values), then the
curse of dimensionality and the empty space phenomenon are once again observed.
These two problems, which spectral dimensionality reduction seeks to alleviate, are
witnessed and so the quality of the embedding is degraded.

As such, care should be taken when seeking to embed a dataset into "higher"
dimensions. The performance of spectral dimensionality reduction methods, and in
fact nonlinear dimensionality reduction methods in general, is called into question
in such cases.

4.5 Summary

This chapter has briefly outlined various approaches to estimating intrinsic dimensionality of a dataset. There is an attractiveness in using an intrinsic dimensionality
estimation that comes as part of a spectral dimensionality reduction algorithm (as
shown in Sect. 4.2. However, this may not always be available as many algorithms

do not exhibit the so called spectral gap property. As such, other methods exist to help obtain an estimate of the intrinsic dimensionality of a dataset. There are however various issues with obtaining such an estimate, such as choosing which algorithm to use and also estimating the dimensionality of datasets with high intrinsic dimensionality. At the heart of all of these issue lies the problem of whether current methods for spectral dimensionality reduction, and indeed intrinsic dimensionality estimation, can accurately and effectively work with datasets where the intrinsic dimension is larger that four or five dimensions. This issue remains very much an open problem, and as stated in [23], only the future will tell if there is a solution to such a grand problem. As well as this, they all work under the assumption that the dataset has a definite dimension [22], in situations where this is not the case, many intrinsic dimensionality estimators will fail to obtain an accurate estimate of the dimensionality of the dataset.

References

1. Nene, S.A., Nayar, S.K., Murase, H.: Columbia Object Image Library (COIL-20). Tech. rep., Technical Report CUCS-005-96. (1996)
2. Strange, H., Zwiggelaar, R.: Classification performance related to intrinsic dimensionality in mammographic image analysis. In: Proceedings of the Thirteenth Annual Conference on Medical Image Understanding and Analysis, pp. 219–223 (2009)
3. Joliffe, I.T.: Principal Component Analysis. Springer-Verlag, New York (1986)
4. Xiao, L., Sun, J., Boyd, S.: A duality view of spectral methods for dimensionality reduction. In: Proceedings of the twenty-third International Conference on Machine Learning (ICML), pp. 1041–1048 (2006)
5. Perona, P., Polito, M.: Grouping and dimensionality reduction by locally linear embedding. In: Advances in Neural Information Processing Systems 14: Proceedings of the 2002 Conference (NIPS), pp. 1255–1262 (2002)
6. Saul, L.K., Roweis, S.: Think globally, fit locally: Unsupervised learning of low dimensional manifolds. Journal of Machine Learning Research 4, 119–155 (2003)
7. Eckmann, J.P., Ruelle, D.: Ergodic theory of chaos and strange attractors. Reviews of Modern Physics 57, 617–659 (1985)
8. Mo, D., Huang, S.H.: Fractal-Based intrinsic dimension estiation and its application in dimensionality reduction. IEEE Transactions on Knowledge and Data Engineering 24(1), 59–71 (2012)
9. Grassberger, P.: An optimized box-assisted algorithm for fractal dimension. Physics Letters A 148, 63–68 (1990)
10. Kégl, B.: Intrinsic dimension estimation using packing numbers. In: Advances in Neural Information Processing Systems 14: Proceedings of the 2002 Conference (NIPS), pp. 681–688 (2002)
11. Grassberger, P., Procaccia, I.: Measuring the strangeness of strange attractors. Physica D 9(189), 189–208 (1983)
12. Camastra, F.: Data dimensionality estimation methods: A survey. Pattern Recognition 36, 2945–2954 (2003)
13. Eckmann, J.P., Ruelle, D.: Fundamental limitations for estimating dimensions and lyapounov exponents in dynamical systems. Physica D 56, 185–187 (1992)
14. Smith, L.A.: Intrinsic limits on dimension calculations. Physics Letters A 133, 283–288 (1988)
15. Efron, B., Tibshirani, R.J.: An Introduction to the Bootstrap. Chapman and Hall (1993)

16. Theiler, J., Eubank, S., Longtin, A., Galdrikian, B., Farmer, J.D.: Testing for nonlinearity in time series: the method for surrogate data. Physica D **58**, 77–94 (1992)
17. Costa, J.A., Hero, A.O.: Geodesic entropic graphs for dimension and entropy estimation in manifold learning. IEEE Transactions on Signal Processing **52**(8), 2210–2221 (2004)
18. Fukunaga, K., Olsen, D.R.: An algorithm for finding the intrinsic dimensionality of data. IEEE Transactions on Computers **C-20**(2), 176–193 (1971)
19. Pettis, K.W., Bailey, T.A., Jain, A.K., Dubes, R.C.: An intrinsic dimensionality estimator from near-neighbor information. IEEE Transactions on Pattern Analysis and Machine Intelligence **1**, 25–37 (1979)
20. Verveer, P.J., Duin, R.P.W.: An evaluation of intrinsic dimensionality estimators. IEEE Transactions on Pattern Analysis and Machine Intelligence **17**(1), 81–86 (1995)
21. Levina, E., Bickel, P.J.: Maximum likelihood estimation of intrinsic dimension. In: Advances in Neural Information Processing Systems 16: Proceedings of the 2004 Conference (NIPS), pp. 777–784 (2004)
22. Fan, M., Qiao, H., Zhang, B.: Intrinsic dimension estimation of manifolds by incising balls. Pattern Recognition **42**, 780–787 (2009)
23. Lee, J.A., Verleysen, M.: Nonlinear Dimensionality Reduction. Springer (2007)

Chapter 5
Incorporating New Points

Abstract This chapter seeks to outline and assess the various methods for the *out-of-sample extension* problem (incorporating new points from the high-dimensional space to the low-dimensional space) and the *pre-image* problem (incorporating new points from the low-dimensional space to the high-dimensional space). As well as this, methods for incremental learning—the process of producing a low-dimensional embedding as new data points appear as opposed to in batch—are discussed.

Keywords Out-of-sample extension · Pre-image · Nyström method · Incremental learning

Given a set of high-dimensional data and the low-dimensional learnt embedding of that same data, how can new "unseen" data points be embedded into that same low-dimensional space *without* re-running the dimensionality reduction algorithm? This question lies at the heart of this chapter. For many problem domains such as classification and regression the answer to this question, and its inverse—how can new points be mapped from the low-dimensional space to the high-dimensional space—is key. Thankfully, the problem of incorporating new points has been an active and fruitful area of research over the past few years.

5.1 Natural Incorporation

As with the problem of estimating intrinsic dimensionality (Chap. 4), some spectral dimensionality reduction methods can be seen to provide a solution to the problem 'naturally'. That is, new data points can be mapped into the low-dimensional space *without* the need for an extra algorithm. The simplest of such methods is PCA [1] which can be thought of as learning a transformation matrix that projects points from the high-dimensional to the low-dimensional space. Recall from Sect. 2.2.1 that PCA computes the covariance matrix $\mathbf{F}$ that corresponds to the amount the data varies in

H. Strange and R. Zwiggelaar, *Open Problems in Spectral Dimensionality Reduction*,   53
SpringerBriefs in Computer Science, DOI: 10.1007/978-3-319-03943-5_5,
© The Author(s) 2014

the high-dimensional space. The eigenvectors, $\mathbf{Q}$, of this matrix describe the principal axes of the data and the d-dimensional embedding is found by projecting the data onto the top d eigenvectors such that $\mathbf{Y} = \mathbf{X}\mathbf{Q}_{1...d}$. What is readily apparent is that since PCA reduces the dimensionality by a simple projection into the low-dimensional space, this projection matrix, $\mathbf{Q}_{1...d}$, can be used to project unseen data points that do not appear in $\mathbf{X}$. Therefore, given a data point $\mathbf{x}^* \notin \mathbf{X}$, its low-dimensional representation can be found by $\mathbf{y}^* = \mathbf{x}^*\mathbf{Q}_{1...d}$.

The natural incorporation of a solution to the out-of-sample extension problem is not restricted to only PCA. What should be clear from the brief discussion above is that any method that uses a linear projection can be thought to naturally provide a solution to the out-of-sample extension problem. A case in point is Locality Preserving Projections [2] the linearised version of Laplacian Eigenmaps [3] or Linear LTSA [4]. Since both techniques learn the vectors that correspond to the projection matrix for embedding the data points into the low-dimensional space, it can be assumed that any new points will not significantly alter this projection matrix and therefore the same matrix can be used to embed the new, unseen, data into the low-dimensional embedding. The key assumption is that the previously seen data, that is the data points used to learn the projection matrix, sufficiently capture the global geometry of the manifold. However, if the data does not sufficiently model the manifold, or if the new unseen data lies significantly apart from the seen data, then the out-of-sample extension method described above will fail to produce meaningful results. It is worth noting that in the case where large amounts of data are to be added to a previously learnt embedding, an incremental learning technique, such as those described in Sect. 5.4, should be used.

The discussion above focuses solely on the out-of-sample extension, where unseen, high-dimensional, data is to be added to be a previously learn low-dimensional embedding. The complement of the out-of-sample extension is the pre-image problem, where the position of unseen low-dimensional data is found in the high-dimensional space. The pre-image problem is not as well investigated in the manifold learning literature as the out-of-sample extension. However, it is a key issue within kernel methods [5] and so many of the kernel methods based solutions to the pre-image problem can be applied to the area of spectral dimensionality reduction.

5.2 Out-of-Sample Extensions

Since most spectral dimensionality reduction techniques do not provide a solution to the out-of-sample extension problem "out of the box", numerous methods have been presented to enable new points to be incorporated into a previously learnt embedding. These methods can be broadly split into those that work for a specific spectral dimensionality reduction technique, and those that are generic enough to work with any spectral dimensionality reduction technique.

5.2.1 The Nyström Method

Perhaps the most well known algorithm specific out-of-sample estimation method is that of Bengio et al. [6] where the problem of spectral dimensionality reduction is phrased within a kernel framework so that the Nyström technique can be used to perform the out-of-sample extension.

In general terms, a symmetric matrix $\mathbf{F}$ is formed from a kernel function K such that $\mathbf{F}_{ij} = K(\mathbf{x}_i, \mathbf{x}_j)$. There then exists an eigenvector and eigenvalue pair, $(\mathbf{u}_i, \lambda_i)$, such that $\mathbf{F}\mathbf{u}_i = \lambda_i \mathbf{u}_i$. The low-dimensional embedding, $\mathbf{y}^*$, of $\mathbf{x}^*$ is then given by

$$\mathbf{y}_k^* = \frac{1}{\lambda_k} \sum_{j=1}^{n} \mathbf{u}_{kj} K(\mathbf{x}^*, \mathbf{x}_j) \tag{5.1}$$

where $\mathbf{y}_k^*$ is the k-th co-ordinate of the low-dimensional representation $\mathbf{y}^*$. This can then be phrased in vector form as

$$\mathbf{y}^* = \left(\sqrt{\Lambda}\right)^{-1} \mathbf{Q}^T K_{\mathbf{x}^*} \tag{5.2}$$

where $K_{\mathbf{x}^*} = [K(\mathbf{x}^*, \mathbf{x}_1), \ldots, K(\mathbf{x}^*, \mathbf{x}_n)]$. Therefore, the Nyström extension maps the new data point $\mathbf{x}^*$ as a weighted linear combination of the previously seen data in $\mathbf{X}$. The full proof, analysis, and justification for this proposition can be found in [6–8].

What is readily apparent from the above formulation is that to obtain a low-dimensional representation of a new point $\mathbf{x}^*$, the kernel, K, needs to be extended. Since the kernels used for spectral dimensionality reduction algorithms are not known functions, extending the kernels becomes a difficult and non-trivial task. The original work of Bengio et al. [6] and Ham et al. [9] provided definitions of the kernel functions to produce kernel matrices for Isomap [10], LLE [11], Laplacian Eigenmaps [3], and MDS [12], which are described in Sect. 2.4 of this book. However, these kernels need to be adapted to handle new points. The adaptions are given in [6] and are detailed below; all are given in terms of expectations $E_{\mathbf{x}^*}$ taken over the original data $\mathbf{X}$.

MDS

The continuous version of the double centring equation (Eq. 2.4) gives rise to the normalised kernel for MDS:

$$K(\mathbf{a}, \mathbf{b}) = -\frac{1}{2}(d^2(\mathbf{a}, \mathbf{b}) - E_{\mathbf{x}^*}[d^2(\mathbf{x}^*, \mathbf{b})] - E_{\mathbf{x}'*}[d^2(\mathbf{a}, \mathbf{x}'^*)] + E_{\mathbf{x}^*, \mathbf{x}'*}[d^2(\mathbf{x}^*, \mathbf{x}'^*)]) \tag{5.3}$$

where $d^2(\mathbf{a}, \mathbf{b})$ corresponds to the Euclidean distance in $\mathbb{R}^D$.

Isomap

The method to extend Isomap to incorporate a new point proposed in [6] does not explicitly recompute the geodesic distances with respect to the new point. Rather, the geodesic distances $\phi(\mathbf{a}, \mathbf{b})$ over the original data $\mathbf{X}$ are used and the j-th co-ordinate of the low-dimensional representation of an unseen point $\mathbf{x}^*$ is given by

$$y_j^* = \frac{1}{2\sqrt{\lambda_j}} \sum_i \mathbf{u}_{ji} (\mathrm{E}_{\mathbf{x}'^*}[\mathbf{D}^2(\mathbf{x}'^*, \mathbf{x}_i)] - \mathbf{D}^2(\mathbf{x}_i, \mathbf{x}^*)) \tag{5.4}$$

where $\mathbf{D}$ corresponds to the matrix of double-centred geodesic distances computed over $\mathbf{X}$ and $\mathrm{E}_{\mathbf{x}'^*}$ is an average taken over the dataset.

Laplacian Eigenmaps

Laplacian Eigenmaps relies on the use of a kernel to define point wise similarities and as such this initial kernel is represented by $\tilde{K}$. With this in place, the extend kernel can be formed as:

$$K(\mathbf{a}, \mathbf{b}) = \frac{1}{n} \frac{\tilde{K}(\mathbf{a}, \mathbf{b})}{\sqrt{\mathrm{E}_{\mathbf{x}^*}[\tilde{K}(\mathbf{a}, \mathbf{x}^*)]\mathrm{E}_{\mathbf{x}'^*}[\tilde{K}(\mathbf{b}, \mathbf{x}'^*)]}} \tag{5.5}$$

LLE

As noted in [6], LLE is the most challenging dimensionality reduction technique to fit within the Nyström framework because its feature matrix, measured as local linear weights, does not have a clear interpretation in terms of distances or dot products. Therefore, a modified kernel is formed in terms of the LLE weight matrix such that

$$\hat{K}(\mathbf{x}_i, \mathbf{x}_j) = \mathbf{W}_{ij} + \mathbf{W}_{ji} - \sum_k \mathbf{W}_{ki}\mathbf{W}_{kj} \tag{5.6}$$

where $\mathbf{W}$ is the weight matrix given by Eq. (2.9). Given a free parameter μ, the k-th co-ordinate of the low-dimensional embedding is then given by

$$y_k^* = \frac{\mu - 1}{\mu - \lambda_k} \sum_i y_{ik} \mathbf{w}(\mathbf{x}^*, \mathbf{x}_i) + \frac{1}{\mu - \lambda_k} \sum_i y_{ik} \hat{K}(\mathbf{x}^*, \mathbf{x}_i). \tag{5.7}$$

A large value of μ should be used so that the above formulation approximates the out-of-sample extension given by Saul and Roweis [13] that is discussed in more detail below.

5.2.2 Generalised

The above discussion of the Nyström extension described out-of-sample extensions for specific dimensionality reduction algorithms with specially constructed kernel matrices. It is unreasonable to assume that such extended kernels can be found for all spectral dimensionality reduction algorithms and as such generalised solutions have been sought. These generalised solutions seek to provide a means of embedding an unseen data point into the previously learnt low-dimensional embedding *independently* of any dimensionality reduction algorithm. As such, they do not require a new kernel to be formed, nor in fact are the solutions limited to spectral dimensionality reduction as they exploit the underlying geometry of the data as opposed to any specific spectral property.

Two generalised methods for incorporating new data points based on LLE [11] were presented in [13], one parameteric and one non-parametric. The parametric model seeks to learn a parametric mapping between the high-dimensional and the low-dimensional space. This is achieved by learning a set of local mixture models that correspond to the joint distribution $P(\mathbf{X}|\mathbf{Y})$ over the high and low-dimensional spaces. By computing the expected values, $E[\mathbf{x}^*|\mathbf{y}^*]$ and $E[\mathbf{y}^*|\mathbf{x}^*]$, new inputs can be mapped from the high-dimensional space to the low-dimensional space and vice-versa. A Gaussian mixture model [14] is used to represent the local linear densities on the manifold. As described in [13], the overall distribution is given by

$$P(\mathbf{x}^*, \mathbf{y}^*, \mathbf{z}) = P(\mathbf{x}^*|\mathbf{y}^*, \mathbf{z})P(\mathbf{y}^*, \mathbf{z})P(\mathbf{z}) \tag{5.8}$$

$$P(\mathbf{x}^*|\mathbf{y}^*, \mathbf{z}) = \frac{|\Psi_{\mathbf{z}}|^{-1/2}}{(2\pi)^{D/2}} \exp\left\{-\frac{1}{2}[\mathbf{x}^* - \Lambda_{\mathbf{z}}\mathbf{y} - \mu_{\mathbf{z}}]^T \Psi_{\mathbf{z}}^{-1}[\mathbf{x}^* - \Lambda_{\mathbf{z}}\mathbf{y}^* - \mu_{\mathbf{z}}]\right\} \tag{5.9}$$

$$P(\mathbf{y}^*|\mathbf{z}) = \frac{|\Sigma_{\mathbf{z}}^{-1/2}|}{(2\pi)^{d/2}} \exp\left\{-\frac{1}{2}[\mathbf{y}^* - \mathbf{v}_{\mathbf{z}}]^T \Sigma_{\mathbf{z}}^{-1}[\mathbf{y}^* - \mathbf{v}_{\mathbf{z}}]\right\} \tag{5.10}$$

where $\mathbf{z}$ is a discrete hidden variable sampled from the prior distribution $P(\mathbf{z})$. The parameters for this model are the mean vectors $\mathbf{v}_{\mathbf{z}} \in \mathbb{R}^d$ and $\mu_{\mathbf{z}} \in \mathbb{R}^D$, the full covariance matrices $\Sigma_{\mathbf{z}}$ and the diagonal covariance matrices $\Psi_{\mathbf{z}}$, the loading matrices $\Lambda_{\mathbf{z}}$ and the prior probabilities $P(\mathbf{z})$. Each of these parameters need to be estimated from the seen data $\mathbf{X}$ and $\mathbf{Y}$. An Expectation–Maximization (EM) algorithm [15] is used to learn the parameters for the above mixture model. The local models learnt using this approach then gives rise to mappings at a local scale between the high and low-dimensional spaces and vice-versa.

The non-parametric model is conceptually simpler as it loosely follows the same steps as LLE. Given a new datapoint, $\mathbf{x}^*$ and a set of previously seen data points $\mathbf{X}$, the low dimensional representation $\mathbf{y}^*$ is found using the following steps. Firstly, the k-nearest neighbours of $\mathbf{x}^*$ in $\mathbf{X}$ are found. The weights, $\mathbf{w}_j^*$, that best reconstruct $\mathbf{x}^*$ from its k-nearest neighbours are then calculated with the constraint that $\sum_j^j \mathbf{w}_j^* = 1$.

Finally, the low-dimensional embedding $\mathbf{y}^*$ is found by $\mathbf{y}^* = \sum_j^k \mathbf{w}_j^* \mathbf{y}_j$ where the neighbours indexed in $\mathbf{Y}$ are the same as those computed from $\mathbf{X}$. As can be seen, this method reconstructs $\mathbf{x}^*$ in the low-dimensional space as a linear combination of the neighbourhood weights measured in the high-dimensional space.

A similar out-of-sample extension solution to the non-parameteric method outlined above is the Generalised Out of Sample Extension (GOoSE) [16]. As with the non-parametric LLE method, GOoSE examines the local structure of the data to obtain a mapping from the high-dimensional to the low-dimensional space. However, unlike the non-parametric LLE method, GOoSE seeks to learn a similarity transform that reconstructs the neighbourhood of $\mathbf{x}^*$ after projection onto its local linear subspace. The low-dimensional representation of $\mathbf{x}^*$ can be approximated in the following way

$$\mathbf{y}^* = \mathbf{A}\mathbf{V}\mathbf{x}^* \tag{5.11}$$

where $\mathbf{A}$ is a similarity transformation matrix and $\mathbf{V}$ is a matrix that projects $\mathbf{x}^*$ into the low-dimensional space. The projection matrix $\mathbf{V}$ can be found by computing the principal components of the k-nearest neighbours of $\mathbf{x}^*$ in $\mathbf{X}$. As such, this projection matrix can be thought of as projecting $\mathbf{x}^*$ into the local linear subspace of $\mathbf{x}^*$ in $\mathbf{X}$. Although this projection maps $\mathbf{x}^*$ into the low-dimensional space it does not embed it into the correct co-ordinate system and as such a similarity transformation matrix $\mathbf{A}$ is learnt. This transformation is found by finding the similarity transform that transforms $\mathbf{V}\mathbf{X}_\varphi$ to $\mathbf{Y}_\varphi$ where φ is the set of neighbours of $\mathbf{x}^*$. Once this similarity transform has been found it can be applied to $\mathbf{V}\mathbf{x}^*$ to find the correct low-dimensional embedding $\mathbf{y}^*$. Although conceptually very simple, GOoSE was shown to be a powerful and fast solution to the out-of-sample extension problem. It is, however, not without its problems, as described in Sect. 5.2.3.

A generalised out-of-sample extension technique that shares much in common with the Nyström methods described in Sect. 5.2.1 was presented alongside a novel manifold learning algorithm called Local Global Regressive Maps (LGRM) [17]. LGRM seeks to learn a Laplacian matrix from the data using a kernel matrix $\mathbf{K}_{ij} = K(\mathbf{x}_i, \mathbf{x}_j)$ where the kernel function takes the form of a Radial Basis Function (RBF):

$$K(\mathbf{x}_i, \mathbf{x}_j) = \exp\left(-\frac{||\mathbf{x}_i - \mathbf{x}_j||^2}{\sigma^2}\right) \tag{5.12}$$

where σ is a free parameter representing the width of the RBF. Given a new data point, $\mathbf{x}^*$, the LGRM framework can be used to embed the new point into the low-dimensional space using the original data $\mathbf{X}$ and its corresponding low-dimensional embedding $\mathbf{Y}$ found using any manifold learning or spectral dimensionality reduction technique. The low-dimensional embedding $\mathbf{y}^*$ or $\mathbf{x}^*$ is found by initially constructing a vector $\mathbf{L}_{\mathbf{x}^*}$ where the i-th element of this vector corresponds to $\mathbf{L}_{\mathbf{x}^* i} = K(\mathbf{x}^*, \mathbf{x}_i)$. The low-dimensional embedding is then given by

Fig. 5.1 A toy case where
the out-of-sample extension
methods described in
Sect. 5.2.2 would fail to work

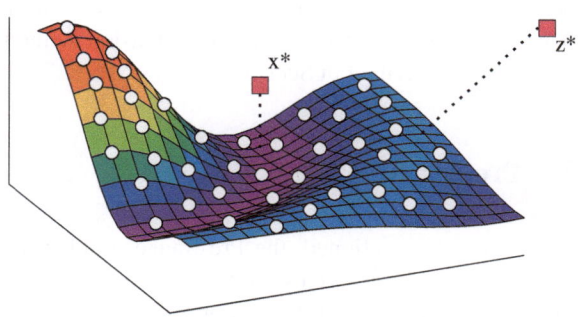

$$\mathbf{y}^* = \mathbf{Y}^T (\mathbf{HKH} + \gamma \mathbf{I})^{-1} \mathbf{HL_{x^*}} + \frac{1}{n} \mathbf{Y}^T \mathbf{1}$$

$$- \frac{1}{n} \mathbf{Y}^T (\mathbf{HKH} + \gamma \mathbf{I})^{-1} \mathbf{HK1} \tag{5.13}$$

where $\mathbf{H}$ is the centring matrix, $\mathbf{1}$ is a column vector of all ones of length n, and γ is a regularisation parameter.

Unlike the generalised extension methods described above, the LGRM method uses the global properties of the data to embed the new datapoint. As such, it does come at a higher computational cost than the LLE and GOoSE methods. It also requires the tuning of a regularisation parameter γ, although experiments do show that a relatively small value of $\gamma = 10^{-4}$ can be used for most experiments [17].

5.2.3 Common Problems

Although numerous solutions to the out-of-sample extension problem have been presented, there are common problems that run throughout the solutions. Firstly, for techniques such as GOoSE [16] and non-parametric LLE [13] that utilise the original high-dimensional data, it is assumed that this data is available; this may not always be the case however. It is conceivable that the data, for whatever reason, is not available and so such methods will not be useable. As well as this, these methods make a fundamental assumption about the unseen data points that may not always be the case and is also difficult to verify. Such methods assume that the new data points lie *within* the previously seen data. That is, the manifold is well sampled around the new data point $\mathbf{x}^*$. As an example of this consider the cases shown in Fig. 5.1. In this example, the manifold is well sampled around $\mathbf{x}^*$ and so $\mathbf{x}^*$ can be reasonably reconstructed from its nearest neighbours. In this instance methods such as those described in Sect. 5.2.2 will perform well. However, in the example shown in Fig. 5.1 for the point $\mathbf{z}^*$ this will not be the case. Although $\mathbf{z}^*$ is sampled from the manifold, it lies far away from any previously seen data points and so its nearest neighbours will not be able to be used for reconstruction. In such cases it may be beneficial to use other out-of-sample extension methods or even incremental learning methods as described in Sect. 5.4.

5.3 Pre-image

As previously mentioned, the Pre-Image problem can be seen as the compliment of the out-of-sample extension. Whereas the out-of-sample extension seeks to learn the low-dimensional representation of an unseen high-dimensional data point, the pre-image method seeks to learn the high-dimensional representation of an unseen low-dimensional data point. This mapping from the low to the high-dimensional space can be particularly useful for shape and image denoising [18, 19], an example of which is shown in Fig. 5.2.

Numerous potential solutions to the pre-image problem have been presented [21–24] but the one of particular interest is that of Arias et al. [18] as they provide a direct link between the Nyström extension for the out-of-sample extension problem, and the pre-image problem. As such, this method fits into the Nyström framework described in Sect. 5.2.1.

As with the out-of-sample extension problem, the pre-image problem is ill defined since the goal is to find the high-dimensional representation, $\mathbf{x}^*$, from a given low-dimensional point $\mathbf{y}^*$. The high-dimensional point $\mathbf{x}^*$ might not exist and so the problem becomes approximating the pre-image so that $\varphi(\mathbf{x}^*)$ is as close as possible to $\mathbf{y}^*$ where φ is the mapping from the high-dimensional to the low-dimensional space. As such, the pre-image problem can be thought of in terms of optimisation where the following optimality criteria is used

$$\mathbf{x}^* = \arg\min_{\mathbf{x}^* \in \mathbb{R}^D} \|\varphi(\mathbf{x}^*) - \mathbf{y}^*\|^2 \tag{5.14}$$

The above is a distance optimality criteria, however, it could also be phrased in terms of collinearity [24] but both are equivalent for normalised kernels [18]. The mapping, φ, from the high-dimensional space to the low-dimensional space can be expressed using the Nyström extension and so Eq. (5.14) becomes

$$\mathbf{x}^* = \arg\min_{\mathbf{x}^* \in \mathbb{R}^D} \left\| \frac{1}{\sqrt{\Lambda}} \mathbf{Q}^T K_{\mathbf{x}^*} - \mathbf{y}^* \right\|^2 \tag{5.15}$$

where $K_{\mathbf{x}^*} = [K(\mathbf{x}^*, \mathbf{x}_1), \ldots, K(\mathbf{x}^*, \mathbf{x}_n)]$ is a vector corresponding to the kernel similarity of $\mathbf{x}^*$ to all other data points in $\mathbf{X}$. This can be approximated as

$$\hat{K}_{\mathbf{x}^*} = \mathbf{Q}\sqrt{\Lambda} \frac{\mathbf{y}^*}{\|\mathbf{y}^*\|} \tag{5.16}$$

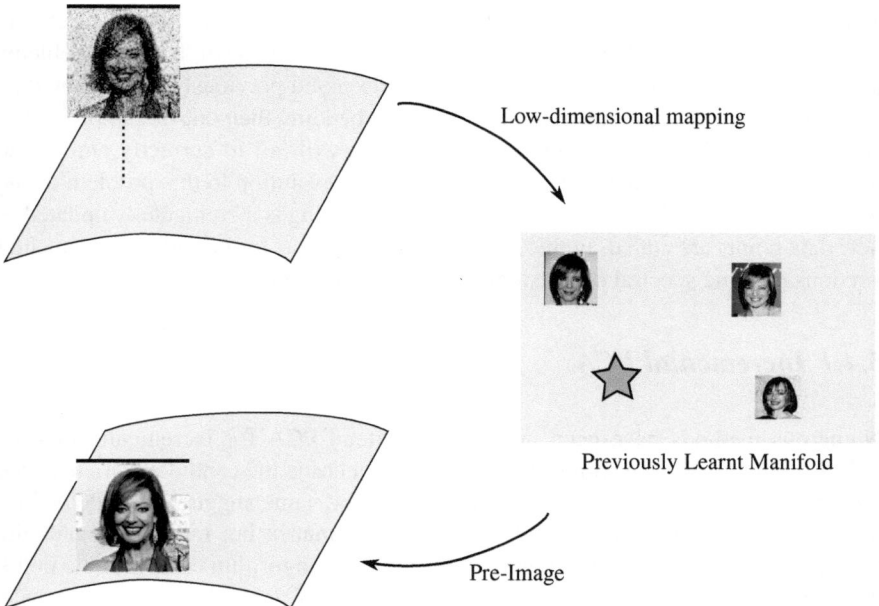

Fig. 5.2 A toy example of how the pre-image problem can be used for image denoising. A noisy sample image, taken from the labelled faces in the wild dataset [20], is mapped into the low-dimensional space of previously learnt images so that it lies on the low-dimensional manifold. The pre-image is then found for this new low-dimensional point to obtain a denoised version of the original image

The pre-image problem can then be thought of in terms of finding closely matching kernel values with the kernel vector estimate:

$$\mathbf{x}^* = \underset{\mathbf{x}^* \in \mathbb{R}^D}{\arg\min} \| K_{\mathbf{x}^*} - \hat{K}_{\mathbf{x}^*} \|^2 \qquad (5.17)$$

The solution to this can be found either iteratively [18, 24] or directly using the direct approximation scheme [21].

The pre-image can suffer from similar drawbacks to the out-of-sample extension, namely the pre-image lying far away from the previously observed manifold. This problem can be partially overcome by providing a normalisation as with the above described method whereby $\mathbf{y}^*$ is projected onto the unit sphere [18].

5.4 Incremental Learning

A closely related problem to that of the out-of-sample extension problem is incremental learning where the low-dimensional embedding is learnt incrementally rather than in batch. Incremental learning has obvious advantages over batch learning, for example, many real world datasets cannot be learnt using a batch learning approach and incremental learning provides an elegant solution for handling such datasets. As well as this, incremental learning can be used to overcome one of the main problems associated with the out-of-sample extensions discussed previously. If the new data points lie far away from the previously learnt embedding then out-of-sample extensions, particularly the local generalised versions, will fail to correctly embed the new data points. Incremental learning can provide a solution to this problem as the low-dimensional embedding and the associated mapping is incrementally updated as new data points are added. In this section, key algorithms for providing incremental versions of some spectral dimensionality reduction techniques are discussed.

5.4.1 Incremental PCA

Numerous methods have been proposed to extend PCA for incremental updates [25, 26] but perhaps the simplest of these approaches is the candid covariance-free incremental PCA (CCIPCA) algorithm [27]. As the name suggests, CCIPCA does not require the re-computation of the covariance matrix but rather estimates the eigenvectors using a fast convergence algorithm. The algorithm computes the first k dominant eigenvectors, $\mathbf{u}_1, \mathbf{u}_2, \dots, \mathbf{u}_k$, from the data $\mathbf{X}$ using the following steps:

1. Let $\mathbf{u}_1(j), \mathbf{u}_2(j), \dots, \mathbf{u}_k(j)$ denote the set of eigenvectors found at iteration j and similarly, $\mathbf{x}_1(j), \mathbf{x}_2(j), \dots, \mathbf{x}_j(n)$ denote the set of data points at iteration j
2. For $j = 1, 2, \dots, m$
3. $\mathbf{x}_1(j) = \mathbf{x}(j)$
4. For $i = 1, 2, \dots, \min(k, j)$

    a. If $i = jn$, initialise the i-th eigenvector as $\mathbf{u}_i(j) = \mathbf{x}_i(j)$
    b. Otherwise,

$$\mathbf{u}_i(j) = \frac{j - 1 - l}{j} \mathbf{u}_i(j - 1) + \frac{1 + l}{j} \mathbf{x}_i(j) \mathbf{x}_i^T(j) \frac{\mathbf{u}_i(j - 1)}{\|\mathbf{u}_i(j - 1)\|} \quad (5.18)$$

$$\mathbf{x}_{i+1}(j) = \mathbf{x}_i(j) - \mathbf{x}_i^T(j) \frac{\mathbf{u}_i(j)}{\|\mathbf{u}_i(j)\|} \frac{\mathbf{u}_i(j)}{\|\mathbf{u}_i(j)\|} \quad (5.19)$$

One of the main drawbacks of the CCIPCA approach is that since the computation of the $(i + 1)$-th principal component depends on the i-th principal component, errors will be compounded and accumulated as the algorithm processes. As such, more detailed and robust methods have been presented to address this issue (e.g. [26]).

5.4.2 Incremental Isomap

The Incremental Isomap algorithm [28] seeks to provide an efficient solution to the incremental learning problem when using the Isomap algorithm. Incremental

Isomap has three main steps: recomputing the geodesic distances; obtaining the low-dimensional representation of the new points; and updating the low-dimensional embedding.

The initial step is to update the neighbourhood graph and then recompute the geodesic distances in light of the newly updated neighbourhood graph. Firstly, the neighbourhood graph needs to be updated since the new data point may change the k-neighbourhood relations by either removing or adding edges to the k-nearest neighbour graph. Once the neighbourhood graph has been reconstructed the geodesic distances need to be updated. The naïve method of doing this would be to run the all pairs shortest path algorithm [29] on the new neighbourhood graph. However, the Incremental Isomap method provides an efficient solution to update the solution to the all pairs shortest path problem. The method involves four sub-algorithms to recompute the geodesic distances in light of the new data point. The full description of these algorithms is omitted here for brevity. Sect. 3.1.1 of [28] provides full details of these algorithms.

The second step is to find the low-dimensional representation, $\mathbf{y}^*$, of the new data point $\mathbf{x}^*$. This can be done using either the Nyström extension method (Sect. 5.2.1), or using a least squares method such that

$$\mathbf{y}^* = \left(\frac{1}{\sqrt{\lambda_1}} \mathbf{u}_1^T \mathbf{f}, \ldots, \frac{1}{\sqrt{\lambda_d}} \mathbf{u}_d^T \mathbf{f} \right)^T \tag{5.20}$$

where $\mathbf{f} = [f_1, f_2, \ldots, f_n]^T$ and f_i can be approximated as

$$2 \tilde{f}_i = \sum_{j=1}^{n} \frac{\mathbf{G}_{ij}^2}{n} - \rho \tag{5.21}$$

where $\mathbf{G}^2$ is the distance of squared geodesic distances and ρ is the distance between $\mathbf{x}^*$ and $\mathbf{x}_i$ in terms of geodesics.

The final step is to update the overall embedding to accommodate the change occurring as a result of the addition of $\mathbf{y}^*$ into the low-dimensional embedding. Due to the increasing size of the geodesic distance matrix traditional incremental eigenvalue methods (e.g. [27] as described in Sect. 5.4.1) cannot be used to obtain an updated embedding. Given the feature matrix $\mathbf{F}_{\text{new}} = -\frac{1}{2} \mathbf{H} \mathbf{G}_{\text{new}} \mathbf{H}$, where $\mathbf{G}_{\text{new}}$ is the updated geodesic distance matrix and $\mathbf{H}$ is the centring matrix, the low-dimensional embedding is found using the following Rayleigh–Ritz acceleration [30] and subspace iteration approach:

1. Compute $\mathbf{Z} = \mathbf{F}_{\text{new}} \mathbf{X}^T$ and perform QR decomposition such that $\mathbf{Z} = \mathbf{Q} \mathbf{R}$.
2. Form the matrix $\mathbf{Z}^* = \mathbf{Q}^T \mathbf{F}_{\text{new}} \mathbf{Q}$ and perform eigen decomposition of the $d \times d$ matrix $\mathbf{Z}^*$.
3. Let $\mathbf{u}_i$ be the i-the eigenvector of $\mathbf{Z}^*$, the updated eigenvectors of $\mathbf{F}_{\text{new}}$ are therefore $\mathbf{Q}_{\text{new}} = \mathbf{Q}[\mathbf{u}_1, \ldots, \mathbf{u}_d]$.

This final step is much faster to compute than the full eigen decomposition of $\mathbf{F}_{new}$ since d is small and no inverse iteration variants are used [28].

5.4.3 Incremental LLE

As with the out-of-sample extension problem, providing an incremental version of LLE is a difficult task as LLE does not have a clear interpretation in terms of distances or dot products [6]. One solution to the problem, Iterative LLE (ILLE) [31], follows the same steps as the original LLE algorithm (Sect. 2.3.4) but with a different eigen decomposition step.

Assuming that LLE has already been run on the original data, $\mathbf{X}$, giving rise to a weight matrix, $\mathbf{W}$, and cost matrix $\mathbf{F} = (\mathbf{I} - \mathbf{W})^T (\mathbf{I} - \mathbf{W})$, the goal of incremental LLE is to update the embedding such that the low-dimensional embedding $\mathbf{y}^*$ of $\mathbf{x}^*$ is incorporated. The ILLE algorithm begins by constructing the cost matrix that incorporates the new data point, $\mathbf{F}_{new}$, by using the traditional LLE least squares method. Once the new $(n + 1) \times (n + 1)$ cost matrix has been calculated, the low-dimensional embedding is computed. It is observed that without loss of generality, the eigenvalues of $\mathbf{F}_{new}$ are the same as those of $\mathbf{F}$. Therefore, if $\mathbf{Y}_{new}$ is the low-dimensional embedding with $\mathbf{y}^*$ included, then $\mathbf{Y}_{new} \mathbf{F}_{new} \mathbf{Y}_{new}^T = \text{diag}\{\lambda_1, \ldots, \lambda_d\}$ given that $\{\lambda_1, \ldots, \lambda_d\}$ are the smallest eigenvalues of $\mathbf{F}$. The new low-dimensional embedding can therefore be computed by solving the minimisation problem

$$\min_{\mathbf{Y}_{new}} (\mathbf{Y}_{new} \mathbf{F}_{new} \mathbf{Y}_{new}^T - \text{diag}\{\lambda_1, \ldots, \lambda_d\}) \tag{5.22}$$

subject to the usual LLE constraints (see Sect. 2.3.4). Since the above minimisation is a $d \times d$ problem it can be solved quickly [31]. The ILLE method does however suffer from the computational burden of reconstructing the weight matrix every time new points are included. Although the computational burden of the eigen decomposition step has been alleviated, the burden of computing the weight matrix for every incoming point can still add significant computation cost.

5.4.4 Incremental Laplacian Eigenmaps

The incremental Laplacian eigenmaps algorithm [32] seeks to incrementally incorporate new data points by adjusting the local sub-manifold of the new data point's neighbourhood. The three steps followed by incremental Laplacian eigenmaps are: update the adjacency matrix; project the new data point; update the local sub-manifold affected by the insertion of the new data point.

The adjacency matrix, $\mathbf{F}$, is initially updated in light of the addition of the new data point $\mathbf{x}^*$. This is done by first extending the matrix so that it is now of size $(n + 1) \times$

$(n + 1)$ and then reconstructing the weights of the samples whose neighbourhoods have changed due to the insertion of $\mathbf{x}^*$.

The low-dimensional representation, $\mathbf{y}^*$, of $\mathbf{x}^*$ is then found by using an alternative formulation of the linear incremental method or the sub-manifold analysis method. Both seek to find $\mathbf{y}^*$ in terms of either the entire weight matrix (linear incremental) or a subset of the weights (sub-manifold analysis method).

Finally, since the presence of $\mathbf{y}^*$ may have changed other data points in the low-dimensional space, the existing embedding needs to be updated. Given the set $\mathbf{X}_{\mathcal{N}}$ containing all the data points whose neighbourhoods have changed as a result of including $\mathbf{x}^*$, the low-dimensional co-ordinates $\mathbf{Y}_{\mathcal{N}}$ need to be updated. This is done by using the two main steps of the LLE algorithm whereby reconstruction weights are measured across the k nearest neighbour of each of the m data points in $\mathbf{X}_{\mathcal{N}}$. Then these weights are fixed so that the low-dimensional representation $\mathbf{Y}_{\mathcal{N}}$ can be found in the low-dimensional space.

The incremental Laplacian eigenmaps method is fast to compute due to its simplicity. It is however dependent on whether the sub-manifold or linear incremental method is used to obtain the low-dimensional representation. The sub-manifold method does provide improved results over the linear incremental method but at an increased computational cost [32].

5.4.5 A Unified Framework

All of the above methods can be unified into a single framework [33]. The unified framework builds on the observation that all of the incremental learning algorithms generally follow three core steps: (1) update structure information, (2) predict low-dimensional co-ordinates of new data, (3) improve previous and predicted co-ordinates. Each of these steps are described below.

1. The first step is similar to the initial step of the incremental Laplacian eigenmaps algorithm [32], where the neighbourhood relations are updated. Given the feature matrix $\mathbf{F}$ obtained using a spectral dimensionality reduction method, the set of data points $\mathbf{X}_{\mathcal{N}}$ whose neighbourhoods change as a result of the new data point $\mathbf{x}^*$ are recorded. This new feature matrix is represented as $\mathbf{F}_{\text{new}}$.
2. The low-dimensional embedding can be given in a number of ways, however, since the unified framework allows for multiple data points to be added at once to the embedding the following proposed method is best followed. The new feature matrix is transformed into a block matrix such that

$$\mathbf{F}_{\text{new}} = \begin{pmatrix} \mathbf{A} & \mathbf{B}^T \\ \mathbf{B} & \mathbf{C} \end{pmatrix} \tag{5.23}$$

The low-dimensional embedding sought is $\hat{\mathbf{Y}} = [\mathbf{Y} \quad \mathbf{y}^*]$ where $\mathbf{y}^*$ corresponds to the predicted co-ordinates of the new data point. It is worth noting that in this discussion only a single data point is considered, however, the unified framework is setup so as to be able to handle the processing of multiple new points at once. The low-dimensional embedding of $\mathbf{y}^*$ can then be found as

$$\mathbf{G}(\mathbf{y}^*)^T = -\mathbf{FY}^T \tag{5.24}$$

3. The low-dimensional embedding of both the previously learnt data, and the newly added data, is then improved using an iterative method similar to Ritz acceleration [34]. The basic premise is to refine the low-dimensional embedding using the updated structure information found in $\mathbf{F}_{new}$. The full algorithm is displayed in Algorithm 1 of [33]. The termination criteria for this refinement step is to either continue for a set number of iterations, or terminate when the error—measured as the Frobenius norm between the previous iteration's estimate and that of the current iteration—falls below a certain tolerance threshold.

The ability of the unified framework to extend an existing spectral dimensionality reduction technique to be able to handle incremental data was shown by providing an incremental version of Hessian LLE [35, 33]. Unlike the incremental methods previously discussed, the unified framework allows for the incorporation of multiple data points at the same time. This has obvious benefits when dealing with incremental learning as it is unlikely to encounter a situation where the new data comes one data point at a time.

5.5 Summary

Most spectral dimensionality reduction techniques do not enable new points to be added to the embedding without using some form of extension. This is because many spectral dimensionality reduction technique do not learn a mapping that extends to any data point sampled from the underlying manifold, but rather learn a mapping that is specific to only the seen data. As such, many of the out-of-sample extension methods use the previously seen data to learn a mapping into the low-dimensional space based on the low-dimensional embedding. Generally, the out-of-sample extension methods will obtain an embedding estimate for a new data point through the weighted combination of previously seen points.

Incremental learning is an interesting area of research within the spectral dimensionality reduction landscape. It allows for new data points to be added to the low-dimensional embedding, in a similar way to the out-of-sample extension methods, but also updates the previously learnt embedding to adapt to any changes that may have occurred as a result of the incorporation of these new data points. Thus, incremental learning is better suited to situations where the manifold is expected to be learnt and updated over time. If the out-of-sample extension was to be used in such a situation then the new embedding would be heavily dependent on whether the manifold was sufficiently well sampled in the original data. If it was not, then the embedding co-ordinates of the new data points will be highly inaccurate. Incremental learning algorithms deal with this situation by incrementally adjusting the embedding to handle the changes in the embedding occurring as a result of the new data.

References

1. Joliffe, I.T.: Principal Component Analysis. Springer-Verlag, New York (1986)
2. He, X., Niyogi, P.: Locality Preserving Projections. In: Advances in Neural Information Processing Systems 16: Proceedings of the 2003 Conference (NIPS), pp. 153–160. MIT Press (2003)
3. Belkin, M., Niyogi, P.: Laplacian eigenmaps and spectral techniques for embedding and clustering. In: Advances in Neural Information Processing Systems 14: Proceedings of the 2002 Conference (NIPS), pp. 585–591 (2002)
4. Zhang, T., Yang, J., Zhao, D., Ge, X.: Linear local tangent space alignment and application to face recognition. Neurocomputing **70**, 1547–1533 (2007)
5. Shawe-Taylor, J., Christianini, N.: Kernel Methods for Pattern Analysis. Cambridge University Press (2004)
6. Bengio, Y., Paiement, J.F., Vincent, P., Delalleau, O., Roux, N.L., Ouimet, M.: Out-of-sample extensions for LLE, Isomap, MDS, Eigenmaps, and Spectral Clustering. In: Advances in Neural Information Processing Systems 15: Proceedings of the 2003 Conference (NIPS), pp. 177–184 (2003)
7. Bengio, Y., Delalleau, O., Roux, N.L., Paiement, J.F., Vincent, P., Ouimet, M.: Learning eigenfunctions links spectral embedding and Kernel PCA. Neural Computing **16**(10), 2197–2219 (2004)
8. Bengio, Y., Vincent, P., Paiement, J., Delalleau, O., Ouimet, M., Roux, N.L.: Spectral clustering and kernel PCA anre learning eigenfunctions. Tech. rep., Département d'informatique et recherche opérationnelle, Université de Montréal (2003)
9. Ham, J., Lee, D.D., Mika, S., Schölkopf, B.: A kernel view of the dimensionality reduction of manifolds. In. In Proceedings of the 21st International Conference on Machine Learning, pp. 47–55 (2004)
10. Tenenbaum, J.B., de Silva, V., Langford, J.C.: A global geometric framework for nonlinear dimensionality reduction. Science **290**, 2319–2322 (2000)
11. Roweis, S.T., Saul, L.K.: Nonlinear dimensionality reduction by Locally Linear Embedding. Science **290**, 2323–2326 (2000)
12. Cox, T.F., Cox, M.A.A.: Multidimensional Scaling. Chapman and Hall (2001)
13. Saul, L.K., Roweis, S.: Think globally, fit locally: Unsupervised learning of low dimensional manifolds. Journal of Machine Learning Research **4**, 119–155 (2003)
14. McLachlan, G., Basford, K.: Mixture Models: Inference and Applications to Clustering. Marcel Dekker (1988)
15. Dempster, A.P., Laird, N.M., Rubin, D.B.: Maximum likelihood from incomplete data via the EM algorithm. Journal of the Royal Statistical Society B **39**, 1–37 (1977)
16. Strange, H., Zwiggelaar, R.: A generalised solution to the out-of-sample extension problem in manifold learning. In: Proceedings of the Twenty-Fifth AAAI Conference on Artificial Intelligence, pp. 471–476 (2011)
17. Yang, Y., Nie, F., Xiang, S., Zhuang, Y., Wan, W.: Local and Global Regressive Mapping for manifold learning with out-of-sample extrapolation. In: Proceedings of the Twenty-Fourth AAAI Conference on Artificial Intelligence, pp. 649–654 (2010)
18. Arias, P., Randall, G., Sapiro, G.: Connecting the out-of-sample and pre-image problems in kernel methods. In: Proceedings of the IEEE Conference on Computer Vision and Pattern Recognition, pp. 524–531 (2007)

19. Thorstensen, N., Ségonne, F., Keriven, R.: Pre-Image as Karcher Mean using Diffusion Maps: Application to Shape and Image Denoising. In: Proceedings of the Second International Conference on Scale Space and Variational Methods in Computer Vision, pp. 721–732 (2009)
20. Huang, G.B., Ramesh, M., Berg, T., Learned-Miller, E.: Labeled faces in the wild: A database for studying face recognition in unconstrained environments. Tech. Rep. 07–49, University of Massachusetts, Amherst (2007)
21. Dambreville, S., Rathi, Y., Tannenbaum, A.: Statistical shape analysis using kernel PCA. In: Proceedings of the IS&T/SPIE Symposium on Electronic Imaging (2006)
22. Honeine, P., Richard, C.: Preimage problem in kernel-based machine learning. IEEE Signal Processing Magazine **28**(2), 77–88 (2011)
23. Kwok, J., Tsang, I.: The pre-image problem in kernel methods. IEEE Transactions on Neural Networks **15**, 1517–1525 (2004)
24. Mika, S., Schölkopf, B., Smola, A., Müller, K., Scholz, M., Rätsch, G.: Kernel PCA and de-noising in feature space. In: Advances in Neural Information Processing Systems 10: Proceedings of the 1998 Conference (NIPS), pp. 536–542 (1998)
25. Oja, E., Karhunen, J.: On stochastic approximation of the eigenvectors and eigenvalues of the expectation of a random matrix. Journal of Mathematical Analysis and Applications **106**(1), 69–84 (1985)
26. Zhao, H., Yuen, P.C., Kwok, J.T.: A novel incremental principal component analysis and its application to face recognition. IEEE Transactions on Systems, Man, and Cybernetics - Part B: Cybernetics **36**(4), 873–886 (2006)
27. Weng, J., Zhang, Y., Hwang, W.S.: Candid covariance-free incremental princiipal components analysis. IEEE Transactions on Pattern Analysis and Machine Intelligence **25**(8), 1034–1040 (2003)
28. Law, M., Jain, A.: Incremental nonlinear dimensionality reduction by manifold learning. IEEE Transactions on Pattern Analysis and Machine Intelligence **28**(3), 377–391 (2006)
29. Dijkstra, E.W.: A note on two problems in connexion with graphs. Numerische Mathematik **1**, 269–271 (1959)
30. Golub, G.H., Loan, C.F.V.: Matrix Computations. Johns Hopkins University Press (1996)
31. Kouropteva, O., Okun, O., Pietikäinen, M.: Incremental locally linear embedding. Pattern Recognition **38**, 1764–1767 (2005)
32. Jia, P., Yin, J., Huang, X., Hu, D.: Incremental Laplacian Eigenmaps by preserving adjacent information between data points. Pattern Recognition Letters **30**, 1457–1463 (2009)
33. Li, H., Jiang, H., Barrio, R., Lia, X., Cheng, L., Su, F.: Incremental manifold learning by spectral embedding methods. Pattern Recognition Letters **32**, 1447–1455 (2011)
34. Stewart, G.W.: Accelerating the orthogonal iteration for the eigenvectors of a hermitian matrix. Numerische Mathematik **13**(4), 362–376 (1969)
35. Donoho, D.L., Grimes, C.: Hessian eigenmaps: Locally linear embedding techniques for high-dimensional data. Proceedings of the National Academy of Sciences of the United States of America (PNAS) **100**(10), 5591–5596 (2003)

Chapter 6
Large Scale Data

Abstract In this chapter the problems of using spectral dimensionality reduction with large scale datasets are outlined along with various solutions to these problems. The computational complexity of various spectral dimensionality reduction algorithms are looked at in detail. There is also often much overlap between the solutions in this chapter and what has been discussed previously with regards to incremental learning. Finally, some parallel and GPU based implementation aspects are discussed.

Keywords Large scale learning · Approximations · Nyström extension · Parallel programming

In recent years the term "big data" has become synonymous with any dataset that is so large it is awkward for conventional methods to work with and conventional algorithms to analyse. The term big data is deliberately vague, what is considered big data in one problem domain may be seen as manageable in another domain. As such, big data, or large scale data, represents an amount of data that is at the limits of usability. In terms of spectral dimensionality reduction, large scale data means datasets that are simply too large (i.e. too many data points or dimensions) for spectral dimensionality reduction algorithms to handle without any extra steps.

6.1 Computational Complexity and Bottlenecks

To understand why spectral dimensionality reduction algorithms often struggle with large data is is important to understand the computational complexity of the algorithms and so identify the computational bottlenecks. Once these bottlenecks have been identified it is possible to provide solutions to help improve performance on large scale data.

H. Strange and R. Zwiggelaar, *Open Problems in Spectral Dimensionality Reduction*, 69
SpringerBriefs in Computer Science, DOI: 10.1007/978-3-319-03943-5_6,
© The Author(s) 2014

The computational complexity can be described as a combination of three separate terms: pre-processing; feature building; eigendecomposition. Referring back to the discussion in Chap. 2, these three terms can be linked to the cost of preparing the data, the cost of building the feature matrix $\mathbf{F}$, and the cost of performing eigendecomposition on this feature matrix. The computational complexity of each algorithm is described in terms of the data, i.e. the number of data points n; the original dimensionality of the data D; the target dimensionality d; and the number of nearest neighbours used k.

6.1.1 Complexity of Spectral Dimensionality Reduction Algorithms

The following sections provide brief sketches of the computational cost of each of the spectral dimensionality reduction techniques described in Chap. 2.

PCA and MDS

The computational complexity of PCA and MDS are perhaps the simplest to compute and describe. Recalling the discussion in Sect. 2.2.1, PCA builds a $D \times D$ covariance matrix from which the eigenvectors and eigenvalues are computed using eigendecomposition. This eigendecomposition is the most expensive operation and can be performed using the power method in $O(D^3)$. Thus, the computational complexity of PCA is dependent upon only the size of the original dimensionality D.

For MDS, the computational complexity is dependent not upon the size of the original dimensionality but rather upon the number of data points n. From Sect. 2.2.2 it can be seen that the feature matrix of MDS is of size $n \times n$ as it densely describes the Euclidean distance between all data points. Since eigendecomposition is performed on this matrix, the computational complexity of MDS is $O(n^3)$.

Isomap

To obtain a low-dimensional embedding using Isomap, three steps are followed: a k-nearest neighbour graph is built; the shortest path matrix of the neighbourhood graph is computed; finally, eigendecomposition of the shortest path matrix is computed. As such, the computational complexity of each of these parts are considered separately before an overall complexity for Isomap can be obtained.

The first step of the Isomap algorithm is the computation of the k-nearest neighbour graph. The choice of nearest neighbour search algorithm will obviously impact the computational cost of this step as not all nearest neighbour algorithms share the same complexity. A naïve search method will have a drastically higher computational cost when compared to a more refined and efficient method. As such, for the remainder of this discussion and the remained of this chapter it is assumed that an efficient neighbourhood search method is used. Specifically, it is assumed that a search method based on the Ball Tree data structure [1] is used. This is not an unrealistsic assumption to make as the Ball Tree data structure is used in many machine learning packages such as scikit learn [2] for the Python programming language. Therefore, the computational cost of performing the k-nearest neighbour search using the Ball Tree method is $O(D \log(k)n \log(n))$, where k corresponds the number of neighbours searched for.

Once the nearest neighbours have been found, the next step in the Isomap algorithm is to compute the all pairs shortest path matrix. As with the nearest neighbour search, there are various algorithms available to perform the shortest path computation. The two leading algorithms for shortest path search in term of computational cost are those of Dijkstra [3] and Floyd-Warshall [4]. If using Dijkstra's algorithm the computational cost will be $O(n^2(k + \log(n)))$ and for the Floyd-Warshall algorithm the computational cost is $O(n^3)$, as such, the best case computational cost of the shortest path search is $O(n^2(k + \log(n)))$.

The final step of the Isomap algorithm is the eigendecomposition of the shortest path matrix, as with MDS the computational cost of this step is $O(n^3)$. Therefore, the overall complexity of the Isomap algorithm is $O(D \log(k)n \log(n)) + O(n^2(k + \log(n))) + O(n^3)$ and since only the most computationally expensive term is being considered the complexity of Isomap can be thought of being $O(n^3)$.

Maximum Variance Unfolding

The computational cost of MVU is similar to that of Isomap in many respects. The first step of MVU is to search for the k-nearest neighbours, therefore the cost of the first step can be thought of as $O(D \log(k)n \log(n))$. Also, the final eigendecomposition is performed on an $n \times n$ feature matrix so the computational cost of this step is $O(n^3)$.

Where MVU differs from Isomap is the construction of the feature matrix **F**. Recall from Sect. 2.3.2 that the feature matrix is built by solving a semidefinite programming problem. One of the disadvantages of semidefinite programming is the possible large computational cost. The computational cost of semidefinite programming is explained in terms of the number of constraints, c, with the overall complexity being $O(c^3)$ [5]. The number of constraints for MVU is $c = nk$ [6] so therefore the computational cost for the semidefinite programming part of MVU is $O((nk)^3)$.

Therefore, the combined cost for MVU is $O(D \log(k)n \log(n)) + O((nk)^3) + O(n^3)$ with the overall complexity being treated to $O((nk)^3)$.

Diffusion Maps

Unlike other global methods for spectral dimensionality reduction, Diffusion Maps does not compute a k-nearest neighbour graph. Rather, the affinities are computed for each pairing of data points, that is, the affinities (Eq. 2.6) are calculated for all points such that the affinity matrix **W** is dense. Since the affinities are calculated for all n points, the cost of computing the affinity matrix is $O(n^2)$. This computational complexity could be reduced by replacing the dense affinity matrix with one that computes a sparse affinity matrix between k-nearest neighbours [7].

Although methods may be employed to reduce the cost of constructing the affinity matrix, the overall complexity of Diffusion Maps is still hampered by the eigendecomposition of the forward transition probability matrix $\mathbf{F}$. As such, the overall computational complexity of Diffusion Maps is $O(n^3)$ as this is the cost of performing eigendecomposition on the $n \times n$ matrix $\mathbf{F}$.

Locally Linear Embedding and Laplacian Eigenmaps

Unlike the global approaches previously described, Locally Linear Embedding (LLE) is a local approach and as described in Sect. 2.3.4 the $n \times n$ feature matrix is sparse. This sparse feature matrix is beneficial as it lowers the computational cost of the eigendecomposition. Specifically, the computational cost of eigendecomposition for a sparse $n \times n$ matrix, $\mathbf{F}$, is $O(rn^2)$ when using specific sparse analysis methods [8]. Here, r is the ratio of nonzero elements in $\mathbf{F}$ to the total number of elements n.

The initial computational cost of LLE is the same as the above global approaches where a k-nearest neighbour search is performed. The computational cost to compute the weight matrix, $\mathbf{F}$, as described in Eq. 2.9, is $O(Dnk^3)$ as this is the cost required to solve a set of $k \times k$ linear equations for n data points [9]. As such, the total cost for LLE is $O(D \log(k)n \log(n)) + O(Dnk^3) + O(rn^2)$. Although the computational cost of performing eigendecomposition is reduced due to the sparsity of the feature matrix, the cost of solving a set of $k \times k$ linear equations for each data point is not insignificant.

Laplacian Eigenmaps is another local technique that exploits a sparse feature matrix. As such, the computational cost of Laplacian Eigenmaps is much the same as LLE with the cost of computing the k-nearest neighbours being $O(D \log(k)n \log(n))$ if using the Ball Tree method [1] and the cost of sparse eigendecomposition being $O(rn^2)$. Here, r is the ratio of nonzero elements in $\mathbf{F}$ to the total number of elements n.

Local Tangent Space Alignment

Although Local Tangent Space Alignment (LTSA) performs eigendecomposition on a sparse matrix, it differs from LLE and Laplacian Eigenmaps in that it computes local tangent planes around each data point. Therefore, eigendecomposition is performed on a per point basis. However, the eigendecomposition is performed on an $n \times k$ matrix [10] and so the computational complexity of this step is $O(k^3)$.

As with LLE and Laplacian Eigenmaps, the eigendecomposition step of LTSA is performed on a sparse matrix and so the overall complexity of this step is $O(rn^2)$. This computational complexity corresponds to the overall complexity of the LTSA algorithm.

6.1.2 Common Bottlenecks

From examining the above discussion on computational complexity it becomes readily apparent that the main bottleneck in spectral dimensionality reduction algorithms is the eigendecomposition of the feature matrix $\mathbf{F}$. Therefore, one of the main goals when dealing with large datasets is how to reduce the complexity of the eigendecomposition. Apart from PCA, all of the above spectral dimensionality reduction algorithms perform eigendecomposition on a matrix that is proportional in size to the number of data points; when the number of data points increases, so does the time taken to compute the eigendecomposition. For very large datasets, this eigendecomposition step becomes intractable. As such, approximations need to be used to obtain an approximate low-dimensional embedding that closely matches the embedding that would theoretically be obtained if using the normal eigendecomposition step.

6.2 The Nyström Method

As discussed above, the eigendecomposition is often the most computationally expensive step. There is therefore a real need to provide solutions that help overcome the computational bottleneck associated with performing eigendecomposition. Perhaps the most widely used method to help reduce the computational complexity of the eigendecomposition is the Nyström method [11–13].

Originally the Nyström method was introduced as a method for numerical integration used to approximate eigenfunction solutions [14]. However, in recent years the method has been leveraged to provide a means of improving the performance of kernel machines [13]. As such, the Nyström method used for spectral dimensionality reduction exploits the fact that spectral dimensionality reduction techniques can be phrased as kernel problems [15]. The basic premise of the Nyström method is to select a small subset of the $n \times n$ matrix and then approximate the remaining subset of the data. As noted in [11], it is useful to describe the Nyström method in terms of matrix completion.

Given an $n \times n$ feature, or affinity, matrix $\mathbf{F}$, a subset size m is chosen so that $m \ll n$. The matrix $\mathbf{F}$ is partitioned as follows:

$$\mathbf{F} = \begin{bmatrix} \mathbf{A} & \mathbf{B} \\ \mathbf{B}^T & \mathbf{C} \end{bmatrix} \tag{6.1}$$

where $\mathbf{A}$ is an $m \times m$ matrix, $\mathbf{B}$ is an $(n-m) \times m$ matrix, and $\mathbf{C}$ is an $(n-m) \times (n-m)$ matrix. In this case, $\mathbf{A}$ corresponds to the affinities between the m random samples, $\mathbf{B}$ corresponds to the affinities between the random samples and the remaining samples, and $\mathbf{C}$ is a large matrix (since $m \ll n$) describing the affinities between all of the remaining samples. Following from the description given in [11], the approximate eigenvectors, $\bar{\mathbf{Q}}$ of $\mathbf{W}$ are given through the Nyström extension as

$$\bar{\mathbf{Q}} = \begin{bmatrix} \mathbf{Q} \\ \mathbf{B}^T \mathbf{Q} \Lambda^{-1} \end{bmatrix} \tag{6.2}$$

and the approximation $\bar{\mathbf{F}}$ of $\mathbf{F}$ is then $\bar{\mathbf{F}} = \bar{\mathbf{Q}} \Lambda \bar{\mathbf{Q}}^T$ which becomes

$$\bar{\mathbf{F}} = \begin{bmatrix} \mathbf{A} \\ \mathbf{B}^T \end{bmatrix} \mathbf{A}^{-1} [\mathbf{A} \ \ \mathbf{B}] \tag{6.3}$$

It is apparent from Eq. 6.3 is that the Nyström extension never requires the large matrix $\mathbf{C}$, rather it implicitly approximates $\mathbf{C}$ using $\mathbf{B}^T \mathbf{A}^{-1} \mathbf{B}$. However, the columns of $\bar{\mathbf{Q}}$ are not orthogonal, therefore a solution needs to be found to find the orthogonalised approximate eigenvectors.

Assuming that the matrix $\mathbf{A}$ is positive definite (If this is not the case, then two steps need to be taken to obtain orthogonalised approximate eigenvectors, as discussed in [11]), then a matrix is introduced:

$$\mathbf{S} = \mathbf{A} + \mathbf{A}^{-1/2} \mathbf{B} \mathbf{B}^T \mathbf{A}^{-1/2} \tag{6.4}$$

which can be diagonalised as $\mathbf{S} = \mathbf{Q_S} \Lambda_\mathbf{S} \mathbf{Q_S}^T$. Given the following matrix:

$$\mathbf{V} = \begin{bmatrix} \mathbf{A} \\ \mathbf{B}^T \end{bmatrix} \mathbf{A}^{-1/2} \mathbf{Q_S} \Lambda_\mathbf{S}^{-1/2} \tag{6.5}$$

then it can be shown [11] that $\bar{\mathbf{F}}$ is diagonalised by $\mathbf{V}$ and $\Lambda_\mathbf{S}$, that is, $\bar{\mathbf{F}} = \mathbf{V} \Lambda_\mathbf{S} \mathbf{V}^T$ and $\mathbf{V}^T \mathbf{V} = \mathbf{I}$.

Therefore, if $\mathbf{F}$ corresponds to a specially constructed kernel matrix for spectral dimensionality reduction as described in Sect. 2.4 and also Sect. 5.2.1, then using the Nyström extension, only the $(m \times m)$ and $(n - m) \times m$ matrices $\mathbf{A}$ and $\mathbf{B}$ are needed to obtain the low-dimensional embedding.

6.2.1 Sampling Methods

One of the key steps of the Nyström method described above is the selection of the m landmark points, often referred to as column-sampling as it is concerned with identifying the m columns from $\mathbf{F}$ upon which the Nyström method will operate. The most basic form of column-sampling is uniform sampling [16], however, more involved techniques have been developed to provide bounds on the reconstruction error of the Nyström method. A proportionally weighted non-uniform sampling method can be applied whereby the i-th column is non-uniformly sampled with the weights being proportional to either the corresponding diagonal element $\mathbf{F}_{ii}$ [17] or the l_2 norm of the column [18]. Both of these methods come at an increased computational cost but diagonal sampling has been used to bound the reconstruction error of the Nyström method [17]. Methods based on adaptive sampling [19] and also on k-means clustering [20] have been presented with excellent results on smaller datasets. However, the ability of the adaptive sampling method to scale to larger datasets is questionable [16].

6.3 Other Approximation Methods

In recent years there have been a number of solutions presented to help alleviate some of the computational bottlenecks for specific spectral dimensionality reduction algorithms. Many of these solutions apply approximation techniques to speedup the most computationally expensive steps of the algorithms. Generally, the solutions will work by identifying a set of landmark points from the data and applying spectral dimensionality reduction to these landmarks. The remaining non-landmark data points can then be propagated to the embedding in terms of the previously identified landmarks. Although the general setting is similar for each of the approximation methods, the specific steps will differ due to the different requirements for each of the spectral dimensionality reduction algorithms. Proposed approximation methods for Isomap, Laplacian Eigenmaps, Maximum Variance Unfolding, and Diffusion Maps, are outlined in the following sections.

6.3.1 Isomap Variants

Two such methods that seek to improve the efficiency of the Isomap algorithm are the Landmark Isomap [21] and Incremental Isomap [22] methods. The basic premise of Landmark Isomap is to perform the computationally expensive calculations on a smaller subset of the original dataset called *landmarks*. Given a dataset $\mathbf{X}$ with n data points, the aim of Landmark Isomap is to work on a much smaller subset of $\mathbf{X}$, $\mathbf{Z}$ where $\mathbf{Z} \subset \mathbf{X}$, $m = |\mathbf{Z}|$ and $m \ll n$. Instead of computing the full $n \times n$ feature matrix $\mathbf{F}$, a smaller $m \times n$ feature matrix $\mathbf{F}_m$ is used which corresponds to the distances between all n-points and the m landmark points. A variant of MDS is used [21] to compute the low-dimensional embedding from the matrix $\mathbf{F}_m$ with considerable savings if $m \ll n$. The computational cost of the Landmark Isomap algorithm is then $O(kmn \log(n))$ for Dijkstra's algorithm on $\mathbf{F}_m$ and $O(m^2 n)$ for the Landmark MDS algorithm.

Another variant of Isomap that can be used to handle large scale data is the Incremental Isomap algorithm [22]. Incremental Isomap was described in the previous chapter (Sect. 5.4) but is briefly reviewed here. The central concept behind Incremental Isomap is to enable the Isomap algorithm to work with sequential data, this means that the entire dataset does not need to be learnt in batch. Instead, the algorithm can learn the embedding in smaller chunks with the embedding changing with the arrival of new data. The application to large scale data should be apparent: given a large dataset, Incremental Isomap could be used to learn the embedding sequentially from subsets of the data thus avoiding performing shortest path search and eigendecomposition on a large matrix. The sequential update algorithm of Incremental Isomap is not without cost, however the cost is still not as expensive as ordinary Isomap. The total cost of update for the Incremental Isomap when using landmarks is $O(\delta \log \delta + q\delta)$ to update the shortest path tree [23], where δ is the minimum number of nodes that must change their distance as a result of the change and q is the maximum degree of vertices in the neighbourhood graph, and $O(nm)$ to update the singular vectors for embedding where m is the number of landmarks used.

6.3.2 Laplacian Eigenmap Variants

Locally Linear Landmarks (LLL) [24] is a recently proposed method that extends Laplacian Eigenmaps to handle large scale data. Although explicitly used to extend Laplacian Eigenmaps, there is no reason why the LLL formulation could not be used to allow other spectral dimensionality reduction algorithms to handle large scale data. At a simplistic level, LLL can be thought of as applying a variant of the LLE algorithm to the entire dataset as opposed to local manifold patches. As with most approximation techniques, LLL works with a subset of the data referred to as landmarks. Again the number of landmarks, m, is considered to be much lower than the number of samples, n ($m \ll n$). LLL seeks to find a projection matrix $\mathbf{Z}$ that represents the data such that

$$\mathbf{X} \approx \tilde{\mathbf{X}}\mathbf{Z} \tag{6.6}$$

where $\tilde{\mathbf{X}}$ is the set of landmarks. This representation can then be plugged back into the regular spectral dimensionality reduction framework but with vastly reduced computational cost since the eigendecomposition is now performed using m landmark points. The two questions which arise from the LLL framework are how to select the landmark points and how the projection matrix $\mathbf{Z}$ is formed. The former question is very much open to the user, a clustering algorithm such as k-means could be used to generate landmark points or a heuristic approach such as the MinMax algorithm could be used [25]. Whichever technique is used to generate the landmark set it is important that the landmarks should be spread as uniformly as possible around the data so as to enable local reconstruction [24].

The formation of the projection matrix $\mathbf{Z}$ is a slightly more involved process. Once the landmark points have been selected, each data point can be expressed as a linear combination of nearby landmark points such that $\mathbf{x}_i = \sum_{j=1}^{m} \tilde{\mathbf{x}}_j \mathbf{z}_{ij}$ where $\mathbf{z}_{ij}$ is a local projection vector and $\tilde{\mathbf{x}}_j$ is the j-th landmark point. The landmarks can be found in a number of ways, however, perhaps the most useful is to use the q-landmark points that are closest to each $\mathbf{x}_i$ where q is the same for all data points [24] and $q \ll m$. Therefore, the projection matrix $\mathbf{Z}$ has only q non-zero elements for every column. Spectral dimensionality reduction is then performed on the set of identified landmarks and the low-dimensional embedding is found via $\mathbf{Y} = \tilde{\mathbf{Y}}\mathbf{Z}$.

The computational complexity of LLL is $O(n(qc + md + Dq^2) + m^3)$, where c is a constant. So although the complexity is cubed with respect to the number of landmarks, it is linear in the number of points n. This is a significant reduction in computational cost when compared to the cubic cost of eigendecomposition.

6.3.3 Maximum Variance Unfolding Variants

As described above, the original MVU algorithm can be very computationally expensive as performing semidefinite programming on an $n \times n$ matrix leads to a complexity of $O((nk)^3)$. Therefore, a landmark approach to MVU has been presented that seeks to decrease the complexity of MVU and thus enable it to be used for a broader class of problems [26]. So called Landmark MVU (L-MVU) seeks to work on a random subset of m landmarks so that the feature matrix $\mathbf{F}$ can be reformed as

$$\mathbf{F} \approx \mathbf{QLQ}^T \tag{6.7}$$

where $\mathbf{L}$ is the $m \times m$ inner product matrix between the m landmarks, and $\mathbf{Q}$ is an $n \times m$ linear transformation found by solving a sparse set of linear equations. To compute the linear transformation $\mathbf{Q}$ it is noted that each data point in $\mathbf{X}$ can be reconstructed in terms of the landmarks through a linear transformation such that for a sample $\mathbf{x}_i$ its reconstruction is

$$\hat{\mathbf{x}}_i = \sum_{\alpha}^{m} \mathbf{Q}_{i\alpha} \tilde{\mathbf{X}}_m \tag{6.8}$$

where $\tilde{\mathbf{X}}$ represents the set of m landmarks.

The semidefinite programming problem is then performed on the matrix $\mathbf{QLQ}^T$. The transformation matrix $\mathbf{Q}$ is derived by a sparse weighted graph whose nodes represents the n data points and the edges are used to propagate the positions of the m landmarks onto the remaining $n - m$ nodes [26]. The use of the smaller $m \times m$ inner product matrix $\mathbf{L}$ allows for an order of magnitude reduction in computation time and also allows for MVU to be used on a previously unusable class of datasets.

6.3.4 Diffusion Maps Variants

As with other spectral dimensionality reduction techniques, Diffusion Maps has a large computational overhead due to the eigendecomposition of a large square kernel matrix. One way to overcome this computational cost is to approximate the final embedding based on a known set of learnt points. Such a method lies at the heart of μ-isometric Difussion Maps [27] (μ-DM). The term μ-isometric maps comes from the fact that μ-DM attempts to find a map $\hat{\Phi} : \mathbf{X} \rightarrow \hat{\mathbf{Y}}$ that approximates the true Diffusion Maps embedding up to some some error μ, that is, $\left| \|\mathbf{Y}_i - \mathbf{Y}_j\| - \|\hat{\mathbf{Y}}_i - \hat{\mathbf{Y}}_j\| \right| \leq \mu$. As with other methods for large scale learning, the μ-DM method works by initially identifying a set of landmark points that sufficiently describe the pairwise distances between data points embedded using standard Diffusion Maps. Once these landmark points have been embedded into the low-dimensional space, a modified version of the Nyström extension—the Orthogonal Nyström-based Map (ONM)—is then used to embed the remainder of the data.

The most computationally expensive step of the μ-DM algorithm is the computation of the pairwise affinity matrix and the corresponding degree matrix [27]. Although μ-DM seeks to construct a subset of the data with only m points used (where $m < n$), the initial affinity and degree matrices are constructed in terms of the entire datasets and as such the cost of constructing these matrices is $O(Dn^2)$.

6.4 Using Brute Force: GPU and Parallel Implementations

All of the above methods use approximations to obtain low-dimensional embeddings of the data and so alleviate the computational bottlenecks associated with spectral dimensionality reduction. One strand of research does not however attempt to find an approximate solution to the problem, but rather uses advances in parallel computing to use computational brute force to obtain a low-dimensional embedding of large scale datasets.

One such method [28] used the CUDA programming language [29], which performs parallel processing over graphical processing units (GPUs), to speed up manifold learning for relatively large scale data. Isomap [30], LLE [31], and Laplacian Eigenmaps [32] are adapted to run in a parallel processing framework. This adaption identifies the core steps of each algorithm, such as k-nearest neighbour identification and shortest path search, and then provides parallel algorithms with CUDA implementations for each of these steps. The spectral decomposition is performed using the CULA library [33] which provides a GPU accelerated linear algebra library.

The results for segmenting relatively small hyperspectral images (128×128 pixels with 200 bands) show that the CUDA implementations provide a speed up of approximately 27 times when compared with non-parallel implementations. Although the speedup is significant, the dataset sizes are still relatively small (the maximum dataset size investigated was $n = 16,384$). What is of more interest is how GPU and parallel implementations could be employed on truly large scale problems.

One of the few studies to use truly large scale data (i.e. $n = 18M$) employed parallel clusters to aid in the computation of the low-dimensional embedding [34, 35]. Although the Nyström method [13] was used on a single machine to overcome the computational cost of eigendecomposition, with a dataset of that size, the cost of computing shortest paths for Isomap and of forming the affinity matrix for Laplacian Eigenmaps becomes intractable on a single machine. As such, a cluster was used to compute the k-nearest neighbour graph and also to approximate the geodesics. Even with a cluster being employed with the spill trees method used, the k-nearest neighbour graph took $\sim$2 days to compute with $k = 5$. The geodesic distances were approximated in 60 minutes.

What is of interest is that even when using parallel processing the time taken to compute the low-dimensional embedding for a large dataset is still prohibitive for many tasks. It will undoubtedly be an area for further research to see if parallel processing methods, in particular those exploiting clusters of GPUs, can be used to quickly use spectral dimensionality reduction on large datasets.

6.5 Summary

Approximations lie at the heart of most solutions to the large scale data problem in spectral dimensionality reduction. By using approximation methods such as the Nyström extension, the computational bottlenecks associated with costly procedures such as eigendecomposition can be alleviated. Although methods have been presented to help existing spectral dimensionality reduction methods to handle large datasets, few studies have been performed on truly large data (i.e. $n > 10^6$). Therefore, an important area of future research will be investigating and developing algorithms to handle such data in a time efficient manner. This will undoubtedly pave the way for spectral dimensionality reduction to be used in a larger class of problem domains where currently the number of data points prohibits spectral dimensionality reduction from being used.

References

1. Witten, I.H., Frank, E., Hall, M.A.: Data Mining: Practical Machine Learning Tools and Techniques, 3rd edn. Elsevier (2011)
2. Pedregosa, F., Varoquaux, G., Gramfort, A., Michel, V., Thirion, B., Grisel, O., Blondel, M., Prettenhofer, P., Weiss, R., Dubourg, V., Vanderplas, J., Passos, A., Cournapeau, D., Brucher, M., Perrot, M., Duchesnay, E.: Scikit-learn: Machine learning in Python. Journal of Machine Learning Research **12**, 2825–2830 (2011)
3. Dijkstra, E.W.: A note on two problems in connexion with graphs. Numerische Mathematik **1**, 269–271 (1959)
4. Floyd, R.W.: Algorithm 97: Shortest path. Communications of the ACM **5**(6), 345 (1962)
5. Chen, W., Weinberger, K.Q., Chen, Y.: Maximum variance correction with application to A* search. In: Proceedings of the 30th International Conference on Machine Learning (2013)
6. van der Maaten, L., Postma, E., van den Herik, J.: Dimensionality reduction: A comparitive review. Tech. Rep. TiCC-TR 2009–005, Tilburg University (2009). Unpublished
7. Mishne, G., Cohen, I.: Multiscale anomaly detectiong using diffusion maps. IEEE Journal of Selected Topics in Signal Processing **7**(1), 111–123 (2013)
8. Fokkema, D.R., Sleijpen, G.L.G., Vorst, H.A.v.: Jacobi-Davidson style QR and QZ algorithms for the reduction of matrix pencils. SIAM Journal on Scientific Computing **20**(1), 94–125 (1999)

9. Saul, L.K., Roweis, S.: An introduction to locally linear embedding. URL: http://www.cs. toronto.edu/~roweis/lle/publications.html
10. Cayton, L.: Algorithms for manifold learning. Tech. Rep. CS2008-0923, University of California San Diego (2005)
11. Fowlkes, C., Belongie, S., Chung, F., Malik, J.: Spectral grouping using the nyström method. IEEE Transactions on Pattern Analysis and Machine Intelligence **26**(2), 214–225 (2004)
12. Nyström, E.J.: Über die Praktische Auflösung von Linearen Integralgleichungen mit Anwendungen auf Randwertaufgaben der Potentialtheorie. Commentationes Physio-Mathematicae **4**(15), 1–52 (1928)
13. Williams, C.K.I., Seeger, M.: Using the Nyström method to speed up kernel machines. In: Advances in Neural Information Processing Systems 13: Proceedings of the 2001 Conference (NIPS), pp. 682–688 (2001)
14. Baker, C.T.: The numerical treatment of integral equations. Clarendon Press (1977)
15. Ham, J., Lee, D.D., Mika, S., Schölkopf, B.: A kernel view of the dimensionality reduction of manifolds. In. In Proceedings of the 21st International Conference on Machine Learning, pp. 47–55 (2004)
16. Kumar, S., Mohri, M., Talwalkar, A.: Samping techniques for the nyström method. Journal of Machine Learning Research **13**(1), 981–1006 (2012)
17. Drineas, P., Mahoney, M.W.: On the nyström method for approximating a Gram matrix for improved kernel-based learning. Journal of Machine Learning Research **6**, 2153–2175 (2005)
18. Drineas, P., Kannan, R., Mahoney, M.W.: Fast Monte Carlo algorithms for matrices II: Computing a low-rank approximation matrix. SIAM Journal on Computing **36**, 158–183 (2006)
19. Deshpande, A., Rademacher, L., Vempala, S., Wang, G.: Matrix approximation and projective clustering via volume sampling. Theory of Computing **2**(12), 225–247 (2006)
20. Zhang, K., Kwok, J.T.: Clustered Nyström Method for Large Scale Manifold Learning and Dimension Reduction. IEEE Transactions on Neural Networks **21**(10), 1576–1587 (2010)
21. Silva, V.d., Tenenbaum, J.B.: Global versus local methods in nonlinear dimensionality reduction. In: Advances in Neural Information Processing Systems 15: Proceedings of the 2003 Conference (NIPS), pp. 705–712. MIT Press (2003)
22. Law, M., Jain, A.: Incremental nonlinear dimensionality reduction by manifold learning. IEEE Transactions on Pattern Analysis and Machine Intelligence **28**(3), 377–391 (2006)
23. Narváez, P., Siu, K.Y., Tzeng, H.Y.: New dynamic algorithms for shortest path tree computation. IEEE/ACM Transactions on Networking **8**(6), 734–746 (2000)
24. Vladymyrov, M., Carreira-Perpiñán, M.A.: Locally linear landmarks for large-scale manifold learning. In: In Proceedings of the 24th European Conference on Machine Learning and Princicples and Applications of Knowledge Discovery in Databases (ECML/PKDD), pp. 256–271 (2013)
25. Silva, V.d., Tenenbaum, J.B.: Sparse multidimensional scaling using landmark points. Tech. rep., Stanford University (2004)
26. Weinberger, K.Q., Packer, B.D., Saul, L.K.: Nonlinear dimensionality reduction by semidefinite programming and kernel matrix factorization. In: In Proceedings of the Tenth International Workshop on Artificial Intelligence and Statistics, pp. 381–388 (2005)
27. Salhov, M., Bermanis, A., Wolf, G., Averbuch, A.: Approximately-isometric Diffusion Maps. Pre-print 2013. URL: http://www.cs.tau.ac.il/~amir1/PS/PDM.pdf
28. Campana-Olivo, R., Manian, V.: Parallel implementation of nonlinear dimensionality reduction methods applied in object segmentation using CUDA and GPU. In: Proceedings of Algorithms and Technologies for Multispectral, Hyperspectral, and Ultraspectral Imagery XVII, pp. 80,480R–80,480R–12 (2011)
29. NVIDIA Corporation: NVIDIA CUDA C Programming Guide (2011)
30. Tenenbaum, J.B., de Silva, V., Langford, J.C.: A global geometric framework for nonlinear dimensionality reduction. Science **290**, 2319–2322 (2000)
31. Roweis, S.T., Saul, L.K.: Nonlinear dimensionality reduction by Locally Linear Embedding. Science **290**, 2323–2326 (2000)

32. Belkin, M., Niyogi, P.: Laplacian eigenmaps and spectral techniques for embedding and clustering. In: Advances in Neural Information Processing Systems 14: Proceedings of the 2002 Conference (NIPS), pp. 585–591 (2002)
33. EM Photonics: CULA Tools: A GPU Accelerated Linear Algebra Library (2013). http://www.culatools.com
34. Talwalkar, A., Kumar, S., Mohri, M., Rowley, H.: Manifold Learning Theory and Applications, chap. Large-Scale Manifold Learning, pp. 121–143. CRC Press (2012)
35. Talwalkar, A., Kumar, S., Rowley, H.: Large-scale manifold learning. In: Proceedings of the IEEE Conference on Computer Vision and Pattern Recognition, pp. 1–8 (2008)

Chapter 7
Postscript

Abstract In this "postscript" a number of aspects are discussed which include how to measure success, non-spectral dimensionality techniques, and also available implementations. The chapter concludes with future research considerations.

Keywords Quality assessment · Non-spectral dimensionality reduction · Manifold learning

7.1 Digging Deeper: How do You Measure Success?

The spectral dimensionality reduction and manifold learning community has seen a large number of algorithms developed over the last decade or so, all of which perform the same task—finding a low-dimensional representation from a high-dimensional dataset whilst retaining important information. One problem that has not been discussed in previous chapters but is of real importance is: given the large number of algorithms available to perform spectral dimensionality reduction, which one should be used? All of these algorithms will display results on artificial datasets as well as some real world data that seem to indicate that the given algorithm can out-perform its competitors. However, the analysis performed is often far from rigorous [1]. The problems associated with analysing spectral dimensionality reduction algorithms can be broadly split into three groups: hyper-focus on benchmark data; lack of appropriate quantitative analysis; data assumptions.

The hyper-focus on benchmark data is a problem that has been observed across the field of machine learning [2]. Typically, a paper on manifold learning or spectral dimensionality reduction will follow a standard evaluation model: the algorithm is applied to synthetic data (typically the swiss role), and then applied to other trickier data sets such as Frey faces or MNIST digits. The use of standard benchmark data is not without its benefits; it allows for a direct side-by-side comparison with other previously published methods and it also makes interpreting these results far easier.

H. Strange and R. Zwiggelaar, *Open Problems in Spectral Dimensionality Reduction*,
SpringerBriefs in Computer Science, DOI: 10.1007/978-3-319-03943-5_7,
© The Author(s) 2014

However, the drawbacks of using benchmark data should also be considered. One of the problems with a hyper-focus on datasets such as the swiss roll is that these datasets are trivial, they do not exhibit the curvature or structure that could be expected from data arising from real world problems. As such, showing that an algorithm can perform well on the swiss roll dataset does not offer any real insights into how the algorithm works or how the algorithm will work on real data.

The second major problem with analysing the performance of spectral dimensionality reduction algorithms is the lack of appropriate quantitative analysis. This is not to say that no algorithms have been presented with quantitative analysis, more often than not a new spectral dimensionality reduction algorithm will be presented alongside some form of quantitative results. However, it could be argued that obtaining such quantitative results is in itself an open problem. Frameworks have been presented to measure the estimated quality of an embedding at a local and global scale (e.g. [3, 4]) and also provide side-by-side comparisons of the stability of various algorithms [5] but these are rarely used when presenting a new algorithm. As well as this, many of the proposed algorithms do not have theoretical guarantees associated with them, which is not always a problem as some machine learning algorithms have poor theoretical guarantees yet work well in practice [1].

The final major problem is associated with the data being learnt as opposed to the algorithms themselves. The fundamental assumption of spectral dimensionality reduction is that the data lies on or near a low-dimensional subspace or manifold. For synthetic data it is simple to show that this assumption holds, however, for data that comes from real problem domains it is difficult to assess whether this assumption is fair or not. The problem quickly becomes cyclic as a 'meaningful' low-dimensional embedding could be used to show that the data lies on or near a sub-manifold, however, the data needs to lie on or near a sub-manifold for the embedding to be obtained. Another assumption is that the manifold upon which the data supposedly lies is embeddable in low-dimensional space. This is a problem that has been touched upon in Chap. 3, but conceivably may not always be the case.

When all of these problems are considered together the question naturally arises: how do you measure success? A similar question was asked with respect to the machine learning field in general [2], and the proposed answer was that results needed to be grounded in real world impact. The same answer could be used for the question with relation to spectral dimensionality reduction. The real success of spectral dimensionality reduction will be measured by how successfully it is applied to real world problems. Application papers are becoming more common with spectral dimensionality reduction being applied to areas such as pathological characterisation of cardiac images [6], image registration, segmentation, and classification [7], fault diagnosis [8], and traffic flow analysis [9]. Undoubtedly, it will be the application of manifold learning and spectral dimensionality reduction to such problem domains that will pave the way for future research in the field.

7.2 Beyond Spectral Dimensionality Reduction

Spectral dimensionality reduction represents a group of common methods for performing dimensionality reduction and manifold learning. They are however not the only methods that can be used for this task. Therefore, other manifold learning methods are briefly described below. As well as this, other applications of some of the fundamental ideas found in spectral dimensionality are discussed, showing that the reach of spectral dimensionality reduction goes beyond just manifold learning for low-dimensional embedding.

7.2.1 Manifold Learning and ANNs

Manifold learning need not be exclusively performed using the spectral framework described in Chap. 2. Other techniques have been presented that utilise heuristics [10], probabilistic formulations [11], advanced optimisation strategies [12], and also artificial neural networks (ANNs) [13]. With perhaps the exception of ANNs, these methods share much in common with the spectral dimensionality reduction techniques discussed previously. As such, they will also encounter much the same problems as those encountered when using spectral dimensionality reduction. In particular, the problems of intrinsic dimensionality and large scale data will be common to all manifold learning and dimensionality reduction techniques. The problem of large scale data has been of particular interest to those within the field of ANN research due to the advent of 'deep learning' [14] which has opened ANNs to be used on large databases [15]. This has been extended into the field of dimensionality reduction with deep architectures being learnt for the purpose of nonlinear dimensionality reduction [13, 16].

These algorithms bring with them their own group of problems that need to be addressed. Although many of these problems are shared with spectral dimensionality reduction techniques, there are some which are unique to their own class of algorithms (such as the choice of optimisation strategy, the number of factor analysers to use, and the guarantees associated with a heuristic algorithm). It is outside the scope of this book to consider these problems, and therefore it is a direction of future research to consider the broader class of problems that encompass all of the manifold learning community.

7.2.2 Beyond Dimensionality Reduction

One of the interesting extensions to the manifold learning and spectral dimensionality reduction problems has been the leveraging of ideas of manifold modelling to other problem domains, that is, the methods used for modelling the manifold are taken *without* the dimensionality reduction step being used. The manifold preserving edit propagation framework [17] is one such example of this. The framework is used to propagate edits made to an image or a video whilst maintaining the manifold structure. The manifold structure is modelled using the two steps of the LLE algorithm. The linear combination of neighbours are modelled in the input space using the LLE neighbourhood weighting method (Eq. 2.9), then these linear weights are reconstructed in the target space to transfer the edits to the new space whilst retaining the manifold structure. This method was successfully applied to colour transfer, image matting, and grayscale image colorisation [17].

Another similar method used Diffusion Maps for edge aware image editing [18]. All operations are performed using the diffusion distance as opposed to the Euclidean distance and so diffusion maps are used to estimate the diffusion distances in the low-dimensional space. What is of real interest is that this is a large scale problem and so the Nyström extension [19] (as discussed in Chap. 6) is used to alleviate the computational bottlenecks. The results obtained using the diffusion distance show that manifold distances can better account for the global distribution of features in the feature space [18].

7.3 Implementations

Perhaps the biggest practical contribution to the field of spectral dimensionality reduction and manifold learning has been Laurens van der Maaten's excellent MATLAB toolbox for dimensionality reduction [20].[1] The toolbox provides implementations of many of the leading algorithms for spectral dimensionality reduction and manifold learning along with some of the associated out-of-sample extension methods and intrinsic dimensionality estimators. There are also functions for generating some of the synthetic data sets that are often used in analysing manifold learning algorithms.

Python implementations of some manifold learning algorithms are available as part of the scikit-learn [21] package. The package provides implementations of PCA, Isomap, LLE, Laplacian Eigenmaps, MDS, LTSA and Hessian LLE as well as providing good documentation into usage of each algorithm.

An open source C++ library for manifold learning is available as part of the C++ Statistical Learning Library.[2] The library contains implementations of some manifold learning algorithms along with other important machine learning tools for unsupervised learning such as k-nearest neighbour search and k-means clustering.

---

[1] Available online at http://bit.ly/9qtyIr (Link checked: October 2013).

[2] Available online at http://sll.sourceforge.net (Link checked: October 2013).

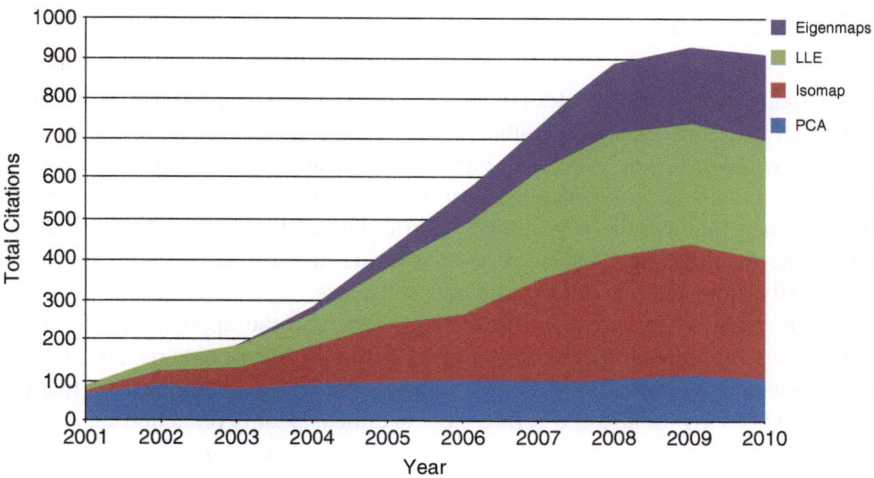

Fig. 7.1 Citations of four of the leading spectral dimensionality reduction methods taken between 2001 and 2010. The citation counts were obtained using the web of knowledge service (http://wok. mimas.ac.uk)

7.4 Conclusions

Addressing the open problems associated with spectral dimensionality reduction is a difficult task as each problem on its own covers a broad spectrum of research. This book has sought to distill each of these open problems while providing an overview of the various solutions that exist to help overcome each problem. Although by no means exhaustive, the discussions in this book should provide enough to enable the problems to be understood and addressed.

An interesting trend within the spectral dimensionality reduction and manifold learning fields is the popularity of the original techniques for manifold learning (Fig. 7.1). Although new algorithms have been presented for manifold learning and spectral dimensionality reduction, by far the most popular and most used as the so-called 'original' algorithms such as Isomap [22], LLE [23], and Laplacian Eigenmaps [24]. This popularity could be accounted for by their didactic value, that is, for many researchers these algorithms represent manifold learning as a whole. However, they are also elegant algorithms which in many cases are as yet to surpassed in terms of performance. The popularity of these techniques means that it is perhaps a more fruitful avenue of research to address the open-problems associated with these techniques as opposed to seeking to develop novel methods for spectral dimensionality reduction. This book has shown that there are still many open problems that still require addressing before spectral dimensionality reduction can be used in various problem domains.

7.5 Future Paths

It is perhaps unsurprising that less and less new approaches to spectral dimensionality reduction are being developed. Rather, research is focusing on adapting and applying existing techniques to new areas. Of particular interest is the application of manifold learning methods to problems outside of dimensionality reduction. That is, the use of some manifold learning algorithm's manifold modelling techniques to problems where the manifold needs to be recovered in the high-dimensional space but not necessarily projected into the low-dimensional space.

Future paths of research will most likely examine the application of spectral dimensionality reduction techniques to real world problem domains. As such, the open problems discussed in this book will become of real importance as many of them will need to be addressed before spectral dimensionality reduction can be used. Therefore, it is expected that rather than new dimensionality reduction techniques, new solutions to these open problems will become a common theme within the manifold learning literature in years to come.

There are various questions that still remain unanswered and will undoubtedly shape future research within the field of spectral dimensionality reduction:

- Is the fundamental manifold assumption a fair one to make for real world settings? If so, how is the success of these algorithms measured? If not, can the spectral dimensionality reduction algorithms be adapted to cope with this new setting?
- Can a mapping be learnt to continuously embed points to and from the high and low-dimensional spaces?
- Are manifold learning algorithms able to successfully embed low-dimensional manifolds into spaces of dimensionality >4?
- Do nonlinear methods actually perform better than their linear counterparts on truly high-dimensional datasets?

It will be interesting to see if these questions remain open, or whether new advances within the field will help researchers to understand and answer them.

7.6 Summary

Although methods exist to address various open problems within the spectral dimensionality reduction research field, such as intrinsic dimensionality and the out-of-sample extension, the problem of measuring the performance of a spectral dimensionality reduction algorithm remains elusive. The manifold learning community has often suffered from a hyper-focus on toy datasets such as the swiss roll which can often hide the true performance of a dimensionality reduction algorithm. To truly assess the performance of a manifold learning algorithm it is important to apply such algorithms to challenging real world problems. Only then will the benefits of using dimensionality reduction and manifold learning become apparent. Thankfully, good and free implementations exist for those wishing to apply spectral dimensionality reduction and manifold learning to their problem domain. These implementations enable the algorithms to be used by a wide variety of researchers and scientists, even those without a formal background in statistical learning theory. The future will show whether spectral dimensionality reduction and manifold learning will be truly useful for a broader class of problems, or whether there are more problems that have not yet been encountered that will need to be addressed before such techniques can be used within certain problem domains.

References

1. Cayton, L.: Algorithms for manifold learning. Tech. Rep. CS2008-0923, University of California San Diego (2005)
2. Wagstaff, K.L.: Machine learning that matters. In: Proceedings of the Twenty-Ninth International Conference on Machine Learning (ICML), pp. 529–536 (2012)
3. Meng, D., Leung, Y., Xu, Z.: A new quality assessment criterion for nonlinear dimensionality reduction. Neurocomputing **74**(6), 941–948 (2011)
4. Zhang, P., Qiao, H., Zhang, B.: An improved local tangent space alignment method for manifold learning. Pattern Recognition Letters **32**, 181–189 (2011)
5. García-Fernández, F.J., Verleysen, M., Lee, J.A., Díaz, I.: Stability comparison of dimensionality reduction techniques attending to data and parameter variations. In: Proceedings of the Eurographics Conference on Visualization (EuroViz) (2013)
6. Duchateau, N., Craene, M.D., Piella, G., Frangi, A.F.: Constrained manifold learning for the characterization of pathological deviations from normality. Medical Image Analysis **16**, 1532–1549 (2012)
7. Aljabar, P., Wolz, R., Rueckert, D.: Machine learning in computer-aided diagnosis: medical imaging intelligence and analysis, chap. Manifold learning for medical image registration, segmentation, and classification. IGI Global (2012)
8. Tang, B., Song, T., Li, F., Deng, L.: Fault diagnosis for a wind turbine transmission system based on manifold learning and shannon wavelet support vector machine. Renewable Energy **62**, 1–9 (2014)
9. Patwari, N., Hero III, A.O., Pacholski, A.: Manifold learning visualization of network traffic data. In: MineNet '05: Proceedings of the 2005 ACM SIGCOMM workshop on Mining network data, pp. 191–196. ACM, New York, NY, USA (2005)
10. Strange, H., Zwiggelaar, R.: Parallel projections for manifold learning. In: Proceedings of the Ninth International Conference on Machine Learning and Applications, pp. 266–271 (2010)
11. Hinton, G., Roweis, S.: Stochastic Neighbor Embedding. In: Advances in Neural Information Processing Systems 15: Proceedings of the 2003 Conference (NIPS), pp. 833–840. MIT Press (2000)
12. Goldberg, Y., Ritov, Y.: Local Procrustes for manifold embedding: a measure of embedding quality and embedding algorithms. Machine Learning **77**(1), 1–25 (2009)
13. Hinton, G.E., Salakhutdinov, R.R.: Reducing the dimensionality of data with neural networks. Science **313**, 504–507 (2006)
14. Bengio, Y.: Learning deep architectures for AI. Foundations and Trends in Machine Learning **2**(1), 1–127 (2009)
15. Le, Q., Ranzato, M., Monga, R., Devin, M., Chen, K., Corrado, G., Dean, J., Ng, A.: Building high-level features using large scale unsupervised learning. In: International Conference in, Machine Learning, pp. 81–88 (2012)
16. Zhang, X.L.: Learning deep representation without parameter inference for nonlinear dimensionality reduction. ArXiv e-prints **1308.4922** (2013)

17. Chen, X., Zhou, D., Zhao, Q., Tan, P.: Manifold preserving edit propagation. ACM Transactions on Graphics - Proceedings of ACM SIGGRAPH, Asia 2012 **31**(6), 132:1–132:7 (2012)
18. Farbman, Z., Fattal, R., Lischinski, D.: Diffusion maps for edge-aware image editing. ACM Transactions on Graphics - Proceedings of ACM SIGGRAPH, Asia 2010 **29**(6), 145:1–145:10 (2010)
19. Williams, C.K.I., Seeger, M.: Using the Nyström method to speed up kernel machines. In: Advances in Neural Information Processing Systems 13: Proceedings of the 2001 Conference (NIPS), pp. 682–688 (2001)
20. van der Maaten, L., Postma, E., van den Herik, J.: Dimensionality reduction: A comparitive review. Tech. Rep. TiCC-TR 2009–005, Tilburg University (2009). Unpublished
21. Pedregosa, F., Varoquaux, G., Gramfort, A., Michel, V., Thirion, B., Grisel, O., Blondel, M., Prettenhofer, P., Weiss, R., Dubourg, V., Vanderplas, J., Passos, A., Cournapeau, D., Brucher, M., Perrot, M., Duchesnay, E.: Scikit-learn: Machine learning in Python. Journal of Machine Learning Research **12**, 2825–2830 (2011)
22. Tenenbaum, J.B., de Silva, V., Langford, J.C.: A global geometric framework for nonlinear dimensionality reduction. Science **290**, 2319–2322 (2000)
23. Roweis, S.T., Saul, L.K.: Nonlinear dimensionality reduction by Locally Linear Embedding. Science **290**, 2323–2326 (2000)
24. Belkin, M., Niyogi, P.: Laplacian eigenmaps and spectral techniques for embedding and clustering. In: Advances in Neural Information Processing Systems 14: Proceedings of the 2002 Conference (NIPS), pp. 585–591 (2002)

Index

H. Strange and R. Zwiggelaar, *Open Problems in Spectral Dimensionality Reduction*,
SpringerBriefs in Computer Science, DOI: 10.1007/978-3-319-03943-5,
© The Author(s) 2014